T0198732

You Can Do It!
(Oh Yes, You Can!)

You Can Expand with Self-Awareness,
Heal with Self-Compassion, and Thrive with
Self-Care Practices That Create Your
Personal Plan to a Happier and Healthier Life

DR. SHEILA BALESTRINO

BALBOA.PRESS
A DIVISION OF HAY HOUSE

Balboa Press books may be ordered through booksellers or by contacting:

Balboa Press
A Division of Hay House
1663 Liberty Drive
Bloomington, IN 47403
www.balboapress.com
844-682-1282

Print information available on the last page.

ISBN: 979-8-7652-3880-6 (sc)
ISBN: 979-8-7652-3881-3 (hc)
ISBN: 979-8-7652-3882-0 (e)

Library of Congress Control Number: 2023901919

Balboa Press rev. date: 02/27/2023

This book is written for...
<u>you</u>.

ACKNOWLEDGEMENTS

I humbly acknowledge and thank
all who have touched my life and
helped bring me to this time.

PREFACE

I wrote this book for _you_.

It's a lighthearted culmination of condensed wisdom and practical steps to a new you.

It's a pocket handbook to happiness!

As a family medicine physician for more than thirty years, I have always felt it was my role to help people to feel better. As a wisdom hunter, my own path led me to discover new ideas and new ways to feel better and expand happiness. I kept picking up pieces of information, writing them down, and, ultimately, fitting them together to renew _my_ life and to create a template for _you_ to do the same.

My desire to explore and understand how health, healing, and feeling better works changed my life for the better, and it can change your life for the better too!

Enjoy the journey!

CONTENTS

INTRODUCTION

Ultimately, the best use of a
physician's knowledge is to teach
people how to heal themselves.
— David Simon, MD

This book is for _you_. Your self-awareness, self-compassion, and self-care practices are vital to your renewed life.

Hi! I'm Dr. Sheila Balestrino. I have spent thirty years board certified in family medicine by the American Board of Family Medicine. I am a physician who has expanded my awareness and my ability to help people outside of the _traditional_ medical office.

I have written this book to broaden my reach in helping people come to new understandings, release limiting impressions, and learn how to create a happier and healthier life! Your health and your happiness _is_ in your hands... and in your heart. It's not as hard as you may think. _You_ can do it!

This book is, on one hand, beyond me. But on the other hand, it _is_ me. It is _all_ of us. It is all of us on our own individual and collective journeys. As a physician, I have written thousands of prescriptions for medications and treatments. In this book, however, I am writing to inspire and encourage your health and wholeness in different ways. Call it a prescription of self-awareness, self-compassion, and self-care practices. These _medicines_ have the ability to promote your own growth, strength, and healing.

In this world, it is our human condition to have forgotten who we really are and to struggle along in the perceived _darkness_ of our day-to-day lives. We have accustomed ourselves to feeling separate from our version of God and separate from each other. Both of these perceptions are painful even in the *best* of circumstances.

In the physical sense, we are separate from each other. Everyone's story and struggle is different. No one has stood in someone else's shoes. We may have shared stories, but each of us has our own unique perceptions, experiences, emotions, and reactions. And it's the unique emotional impressions that we register and accrue that impact our behavior, our health, and our whole lives.

As a physician, I have come to recognize that addressing these emotional impressions is vital to successful health and the promotion of healing. Often, your body is trying to tell you that something is beneath your symptoms that needs attention. While traditional medicine and treatments can be effective, they can *overlook* an important underlying contribution to the problem, illness, or disease. Maybe some changes need to be made at the *root level*. This may include a release of stored emotional impressions that have grown *roots* in our lives. Just like a weed in the soil, if you just treat the surface symptoms of an illness (cut off the top of the weed) and neglect the root contributions (the root), the issues will likely recur in a different time or form. In other words, the weed regrows.

> We need to address the biography
> beneath the biology.
> — David Simon MD, *Free to Love, Free to Heal*

It's the release of these emotional impressions that brings relief, a new perspective, and a new way to grow and flourish.

In this book, I will lead you to find your way through life's maze of struggle and suffering to a place where you can feel happier and healthier.

Renewed self-awareness *is* possible. You will find this is part one.

Healing through self-compassion *is* possible. You will find this in part two.

A self-care practice that creates a better life *is* possible. You will find this in part three.

> Everything is possible for one who believes.
> — Jesus, Mark 9:23 (New International Version)

You become what you believe.

- Why not *believe* that life *doesn't* have to be so hard?
- Why not *believe* that you are *not lost* or alone?
- Why not *believe* that you are *not* separated from God/Source?
- Why not *believe* that you are *not defined* by the way the world defines you?
- Why not *believe* that you *can* change and improve your mind, emotions, and body?
- Why not *believe* that you *can* create a new way of thinking, feeling, and living that is enjoyable, peaceful, and healthy?

This sounds like a win-win situation to me. This *is* possible. You can do it!

It matters not who you are, who you have been, where you are from, what you have, or what you have not done. All players are equal—no judgement here. You can start wherever you are. If you're standing in the mud of life, I'll stand there with you. Then I'll offer you some guidance and tools to take steps forward onto the bank where you can start to walk more easily in a direction of strength and contentment. (We'll wash some of that mud off too.)

I'm not going to say it's without personal effort. I *am* saying, however, that it's worth the effort and persistence it takes to get to a new place—a happier, healthier, and better feeling place.

There is no right or wrong, and there is no time clock. You can choose to release and change what you want and when you want.

How you do it might be different than what you might think.

You only need a *desire* to feel better, a *willingness* to receive, and a *belief* that it *is* possible. If you can only partially commit to this, I will be the rest of it with you.

—I have a desire, a will, and a passion to help you feel better and to live better.

—I believe that it *is* possible.

—I *know* that it's possible.

I have found the way out of the mud of life's pain and struggles, and I've come here to the maze and the mud to find you and help you to find your way out too.

This book is written as a gentle virtual journey through your life's maze and to the clearing and freedom of a happier, healthier you.

This adventure is weaved with love and compassion, inspiring quotes and pearls of wisdom, heartfelt music, and strength for each day. It's a collaboration of love… that has come for You.

So, come on! Let's go!
You can do It!
(Oh yes, you can!)

Musical Offering

"Dive" by Steven Curtis Chapman
"Dare You to Move" by Switchfoot

Pearl

You can do this!

PART ONE

Rx

Name _____ You _____ .

Date _Today_ .

Self-Awareness

Refills _Yes_ .

S. Balestrino D.O.

You Are Here...

Come on, let's go!

CHAPTER 1

Yes, Life Is Hard, But...

*Adversity can be an opportunity for us to
know, accept, and love ourselves more deeply.*

Great job! You turned the page. You're ready to get started on creating a new and improved way of living. OK, even if you're not *fully* ready, you're at least curious. I'll take curious. Curious is good. Remember, I'm here with you. I'm leading you through this maze and out the other side.

First, let's just say it: "Life is hard!" Yes, there is pain, sorrow, loss, and confusion. There's even anxiety, fear, mistreatment, and betrayal. You can add your own items to the list too. We can experience all of these emotions in so many different ways and combinations. It can seem endless, actually.

People often say, "No one said it would be easy." I think those people got it right. Navigating life is not easy. I think the word *easy* means no problems, no negative emotions to feel, and no negative experiences to have to plunder through and navigate. So the quicker we drop the idealism that life *should* be easy, always comfortable, or different than it is, the better off we will be.

I suspect many of us think life *should* be easier. Sometimes we aren't even aware that we feel that way. We just experience life as a struggle, and we become confused and annoyed. Sometimes the unconscious feelings become conscious, and we hear ourselves blurt out, "Why is this so hard?" Have you ever done something like that? I know I have.

When we come to the place where we realize life *is*, indeed, difficult, it somehow feels a bit easier. You may think, *Oh, it's supposed to be this way. I didn't get a raw deal. It's not easy for anyone. I also acknowledge that there is a broad spectrum of human pains and struggles.*

I am so sorry for anyone's personal, emotional, and physical suffering on any level. We all feel what we feel and experience what we experience. The answers to the question *why?* don't always come. Those shoes over there in the *greener* grass may not feel as comfortable as you think. Everyone is working through and creating his or her own experiences, so try not to compare your issues to anyone else's because each person's issues are unique and their own.

Laundry / Cleaning / Yard Work / Jobs

Simplistically, life is like laundry, housecleaning, yard work, and our many other jobs. It's *never* done, so ease up. You're not behind. Don't worry or dread that more is coming. Yes, there *is* more coming. It's a big circle. But you can still feel good when you complete a task. The laundry is done. The yard is mowed. Pump your fist and pat yourself on the back! Just try not to spend any time and energy dreading that the work may return again because it will.

Realistically, the bills return, issues of childcare surface, a health issue pops up, a loved one passes, or a relationship ends. Life is full of changes that we must accept, feel our way through, and manage. Acknowledge what you have done and what you have learned on your way through. "I paid the bills. I made it through the loss. I'm still OK. I feel better. I didn't sabotage myself!"

We are all here to experience and navigate our way through this experience called life. Perseverance is required. Help is required. We aren't meant to do this alone.

Life can feel like one hurdle after another, and sometimes it can feel like a maze. On some days, it can even feel like a combination of the two. I have even felt like just when I found a clearing in my path, the maze changed just to frustrate me. Just like that staircase moving in a *Harry Potter* movie. Yikes!

Just when you think you have a foothold, something else pops up and you're diverted again. You may wonder, *Why is this so hard?* The laundry has returned. The grass in the yard has grown back. Life *is* that circle.

But it's not meant to be a never-ending circle of pain and struggle. There can also be good times of relief, happiness, rest, wonder, peace, fun, contentment, exploration, triumph, and growth. These are in the mix, so enjoy and celebrate them. We can even choose to extend their stays. More on this is coming.

The Stream

Another life analogy is that of a stream. This sounds peaceful. Deepak Chopra[1] and Esther Hicks[2] have each explained this well in their writings, audios, and videos, which I will combine and paraphrase.

When we really look at it, there are two main categories of emotions and experiences. There is love/pleasure and fear/pain. Let's put love/pleasure on the left shore of the stream and fear/pain on the right.

We are navigating the stream of life in a canoe, a boat, or whatever suits you. The currents of life and the rocks (seen and unseen) will take you in different directions. Sometimes, you move a little left, and sometimes, you feel a big thrust right. You will even bump into the shores for periods of time. As humans, we can experience the full spectrum of emotions.

We can feel many emotions in just one day. We can feel loved in the morning, feel frustrated and confused midday, and then feel comforted in the evening. It's all OK. We are here to feel, express, and experience whatever comes our way.

To suppress our feelings can be limiting and hurtful and often promote emotional strife and physical illness. If, by chance, your canoe bumps into a big rock of life and you feel angry, scared, or sad, you have drifted close to the shore on the right. And it's OK. But try not to stay there too long, or you may end up stuck in the mud and docked to bitterness and depression. That is not good. Again, don't deny how you feel. Let's deal with it.

Dealing With It

Deal with how you feel. First, you need to be fully aware of how you are feeling and acknowledge it. If an example of how you have felt or are currently feeling is bubbling up now, you can go ahead and let it out here by writing it down on the line below, if you like.

_____

_____

Second, take a step back from yourself and see yourself from a few feet away. Have compassion for yourself and maybe even write down what you are feeling for yourself below.

_____

_____

_____

Many wise ones have said, "You have to feel it to heal it." Once you're aware of and have acknowledged how you are feeling, you can choose to change it. Yes, you can change it. How long do you want to hang on to a negative feeling? Low self-esteem, sadness, resentment, unforgiveness, and depression all hurt and limit you. If you hang on too long, it will become a dominant focus. It will become *mud* and will poison your time and your life with more bad feelings.

But if you can choose to let go, and then choose how you would prefer to feel, you can push away from the shore on the right. You can change your feelings by changing your thoughts and perceptions to ones that help you feel better. You can only control you. "This is what happened, and this is how I feel. I now have a choice in how I respond for my well-being." Self-compassion will help you release some of the mud. We will talk about this in part two.

You can find or restore peace, contentment, and more. It takes self-care and some practice, but you can do it!

In regard to the stream, you might think that it is best to be docked to the left shore. But not so fast. Actually, staying too long on either shore is not in our best interest. Seeking, choosing, or demanding only pleasurable experiences can lead to struggle, disappointment, and even addictions. Sorry, but bliss, perfection, and peak experiences don't last indefinitely—at least not in an active human experience.

It is best, then, to try to navigate toward the center of the stream most of the time. It feels like contentment.

Upstream/Downstream

Another concept to consider, within the analogy of the stream of life, are our thoughts, as we float along. Specifically, do you choose upstream or downstream thoughts? Our thoughts create our emotions. What you think about, how you think about it, and how long you think about it affects how you feel.

Downstream thoughts are neutral or positive:

- This is good.
- I am OK, and I can make it.
- Everything will work out.
- I am enough just as I am.
- I am worthy and supported.
- I can choose again.
- I accept what is.

When we are floating downstream, we don't even need to use the oars. We flow with the currents of life.

Upstream thoughts, however, are different. Struggle is involved. We have actually turned the canoe around and are paddling upstream, against the current. There is resistance and turbulence.

- Life is too hard.
- I can't make it.
- I'm not enough.
- Things never work out for me.
- I am alone and unsupported.
- Add your own here:

So we navigate the stream of life with the thoughts we choose. You choose them; I choose them; we all choose them. And when you and I are choosing our thoughts, we are choosing our emotions. Again, we will discuss more about this in part two.

> I am the master of my fate. I am
> the captain of my soul.
> — William Ernest Henley

We are the captains of our canoes (or boats or ships)! We get to choose. How do you *prefer* to feel? Upstream thoughts create upstream feelings. Downstream thoughts bring you downstream feelings. Once you become aware of which direction your canoe is headed, you can redirect yourself to a better-feeling place if you like. Redirect, and practice your focus of better feelings.

By the way, *you* are not your thoughts. You have thoughts and emotions. Emotions are just moments of energy in motion. You are neither of these. You are not defined by your thoughts, feelings, or external circumstances. You are not what you have, have done, or own. You are not your reputation, your titles, or defined by how others treat you. Your soul, your inner true self, is the captain navigating the often-rough waters we call life.

Your true self came here to navigate, to experience, and to grow. It's a process. We are all works in progress. But it's a process and a journey that you never travel alone. Thank God/the Universe for that.

Wait … You know that, right? You know that you are not alone, right?

OK. Come this way…Turn here.

Musical Offering

"It's a Hard Love" by Need to Breathe
"Never Too Far Gone" by Jordan Feliz
"Something Wild" by Lindsey Stirling

Pearl

Life is a process that you can
change for the better.

CHAPTER 2

You Are Not Lost, and You Are Never Alone

If you knew who walked beside you at all times, on the path that you have chosen, you could never experience fear or doubt again.
—Dr. Wayne W. Dyer[3]

No. You are not lost. You have never been lost, and you have never been alone, although I certainly would not blame you for feeling lost or alone at times. I understand. Life's challenges can make you feel separate from others and even isolated at times. I am very sorry if you have ever felt lost and/or alone. It's a bad feeling no matter the degree to which you feel it or in whatever the particular experience. Stay with me here... Let's keep walking forward.

A Walk to Oz

Do you remember dear Dorothy from *The Wizard of Oz*?[4] Dorothy felt so lost and so alone (well, mostly) when she woke up in Munchkinland. At first, it seemed like a bright and happy place. It was colorful and full of wonder and joyful little people. What's not to like?

Well, as you know, the story changes. Contrast shows up. Enter the Wicked Witch of the West—yikes. (That green face with the pointy chin still haunts me!) She was pretty mad when Glinda the Good Witch of the South put her sister's ruby slippers on Dorothy's feet. Now Dorothy had to leave town—and fast. She had to leave the beauty and the wonder of her new happy existence. She was off to explore the unknown on a journey to find the Wizard of Oz.

Dorothy set off on a crazy maze of a path made of yellow bricks. She set out for the land of Oz in order to find her way back home to Kansas. In Kansas, she felt safe and loved by her family and friends. She knew who she was, and she knew everyone around her. She felt secure and connected. She felt contentment and peace there.

Life is not unlike Dorothy's predicament. We get dropped off in this physical world from our spiritual source (the big Kansas). We then have to experience our new surroundings. We have to comprehend it, adjust, think, feel, make choices, react, and keep going.

At first, our souls are likely just happy. We want to love and be loved, communicate with others, and experience all there is to experience.

It sounds simple enough. Soon, however, we encounter others who have been around here for a while and have developed their own patterns of living. They have learned how to navigate the lives they were exposed to in their own generations. They learned to conform (or to not conform) to the impressions that others, society, and local culture modeled for them. They had their own impressions, perspectives, ideas, and choices. These were our family members, neighbors, caregivers, and communities.

As we interact with others, we interpret their care, intentions, and behaviors. We then react to what we interpret and learn new patterns of being. As we grow, we learn what to do to feel accepted, loved, and praised. We also learn what not to do to avoid disappointment, disapproval, pain, or rejection.

That initial peaceful and content state of the soul that we were all born with is similar to being in the eye of a tornado. It feels pretty good there with no harsh winds or turmoil. But the tornado of physical life surrounds us. It's hard to stay in the eye of the storm when we experience life's twists and turns. We may experience fear, neglect, rules, standards, pain, sadness, or even misperceptions that pull us over toward the funnel cloud with the rest of humanity.

We do the best we can as we navigate the winds of this life. The winds of time and experience are very strong, and we are eventually drawn over into the funnel cloud. As time goes on, we usually forget about the peaceful eye of the storm that we once knew. We gradually adjust to the winds of life. But this sense of amnesia, over time, can feel like a crash landing. Yep—it's Munchkinland. We're not in Kansas anymore.

And so it begins. A sense of separateness and maybe even disconnection has set in. The yellow brick road is before you. The ego that has developed (your smaller, life-story self) has stepped in to navigate for the soul, and you don't even realize it.

This amnesia of our soul, let the ego go on to define us and the story of our lives. We take off on the road of identifying ourselves, others, and the world based on our thoughts, feelings, judgements, perceptions, and experiences.

We all develop our own unique understanding of ourselves and of the world. Am I good, or am I bad? Am I safe, or am I unsafe?

Who Am I ?

Eckhart Tolle teaches us in the book *A New* Earth[5] that the more you make your thoughts into your identity, the more you are cut off from your true spiritual self. He goes on to explain that the truth is that you are not the thinker, but you are actually the awareness *behind* your thoughts, words, and voice. Got it? You are a soul; that inner true self.

OK, come back to Oz with me. We catch up with Dorothy, and we find her first encountering dear Scarecrow—poor guy. He just couldn't think straight. It seemed as if the more he tried to think straight, the more he struggled.

Struggle leads to more struggle. The more we label, judge, and react, the more we get entangled with the ego and our identities in the world—ego quicksand. Eckhart Tolle calls this "identification,"

The ego self-concept is always identified with the physical form, material objects, one's appearance or abilities, and one's thoughts. You may not even realize that you have attached your identity to something until it is lost or threatened by loss. You may experience stress when you lose something or someone that you have made a part of your identity. This is your ego identity self-concept. Some call it your small self. Remember your big self? That's your soul.

Back to Oz

So, returning to our characters … Dorothy and Scarecrow could not think their way home. Everything was new and unfamiliar. The farther they traveled, the more lost and alone they felt, but they just kept moving forward.

That's what we do, right? We keep striving, pushing, and sometimes coasting forward. We skip, we walk, and, occasionally, we crawl. When the pace picks up, we can run and even climb if we need to.

Along the way, we may lose heart and feel sadness, regret, stress, fatigue, depression, or even defeat. This is where we insert the question: "Why is life so hard?" It is *not* easy. No one said it would be.

Is it all a struggle? Certainly not. Good days and good feelings are in the mix, but we came here to experience the contrast of the human existence. Panache Desai[6] had me laughing when he described Earth as a Vrbo rental property or a fixer-upper. We left the Ritz Carlton for a while. It gets easier if we realize this and just stop expecting or demanding that everything goes our way.

Also, it's best not to expect or demand everyone else to be on the same page of personal growth that we are. Everyone is fixing up their own lives. Some of them bump into us. Some of them are loud or grumpy, while others are kind and happy. We are all trying to learn how to love ourselves and each other better, but we have just forgotten. Earth really *is* a beautiful place. Make a point to look around and focus on the good. So, let's keep moving.

Now, as you remember in the story, as the two make their way to find the Wizard of Oz, Scarecrow comes across the rusted and worn Tin Man. He didn't have a heart. Or did he lose it along the way? He couldn't feel love or loved. He needed a squirt from the oil can just to talk and move. Have you ever felt that way? I have. We all need some support in our lives.

Sometimes, when life's circumstances occur, we can become confused and even overwhelmed with negative emotions. We may not even realize that it's happening. We just react. But the more we align with the struggle, the more it entangles us. Then we begin to believe that it's a part of who we are. We let the many feelings of struggle define us and say things like, "I can't do this! I can't make it!" This can become a pattern over time. It becomes familiar. When we repeat negative patterns, like raindrops on metal, we create our own rust.

Have you ever lost heart and rusted? We all need the healing oil of love and compassion to free us, untangle us, and reawaken our hearts so that we can move forward again. That love is always available and flowing through you, me, and everyone else. Love is our natural state, and it is what and who we are. We simply need to remove the rust to feel it.

From Fear to Love

So, just what is healing anyway? It's the relief we experience as we shift from fear to love. Love is who we are. As Anita Moorjani,[7] author and speaker who had a near-death experience, has said, we are all threads of love in the tapestry of creation. As such, we are unique and valuable to the whole. The ego (the smaller, life-story self), sometimes uses fear to support itself and resist change. We just need to step back and be aware to reevaluate our choices.

Speaking of fear… Enter Cowardly Lion. We all loved him even though he was completely overtaken with worry, self-doubt, and intense fear. Remember when he was so afraid to meet the Wizard that he turned around, ran down the corridor, and jumped out of the window?! Poor guy.

I think we've all experienced fear in some form or another and in different degrees. All that does not fall into the category of love is a form of fear. Fear can feel like resistance. It's a form of friction that can get in the way of experiencing our true nature which is peace.

Our beliefs, thoughts, emotions, and actions can be driven by or even controlled by fear if we allow it. The core fears that limit us are the thoughts and emotions that often funnel down to these statements: "I am not enough." And, "I am unlovable."

Ouch. Unfortunately, if we feel this way, we can unwisely seek relief from our discomforts in a myriad of numbing habits or addictions. These choices can only take us further away from the comfort of love and wholeness that we desire. I have heard it said that whatever you are running from you carry with you, and whatever you are looking for is within you. Wherever you go, there you will be.

Addictions and unhealthy habits have negative consequences and bring feelings of guilt (what I did was bad) and shame (I am bad), which only takes us further away from remembering our value and wholeness. Here are some examples of numbing agents that can escalate:

- overstriving
- mindless television or tech time
- overthinking
- compulsive shopping
- gambling
- overeating
- excessive caffeine or sugar use
- drug and alcohol use
- a negative mindset

> Dessert, television, and sex serve their
> purpose, but when they become substitutes

> for connection to self and others, they
> divert you from the happiness you seek.
> —Alan Cohen, *A Course in Miracles Made Easy*[8]

Inclinations and impulses can become well-worn patterns. How do we change them? In order to change anything, we first need to see what we are doing—*awareness*. It's actually our awareness and remembrance of who we really are that releases the grip of unhealthy habits and addictions. And when you are aware of your truth, you can then take productive steps to release and heal old impressions and patterns and create new, healthier ones.

You Have A Choice

You can choose to change your focus to healthier, more loving behaviors—preferably, those you enjoy! What you focus on gets bigger. What do you enjoy doing that would promote a healthy balance? Do you like to read, exercise, paint, fish, hike, eat out, play a sport, or help others? Choose what suits you and *do* them. Develop a new routine. Practice and repeat. The old habits that seemed to dominate you will fade and recede in the light of your new healthy practices and mindset.

Then notice how much better you feel when you let go of painful emotions and habits and replace them with compassionate self-care. A sense of peace is your reward. Old tapes are replaced with an inner sense that tells you: "I am enough." And, "I am lovable."

The choices are yours. Do you want to struggle and suffer, or do you want to make some adjustments to feel better? Will the speed bumps of life come anyway? Sure they will. But you will be better equipped to handle them. An unexpected expense pops up, a career change, a threatened relationship, a physical illness, or an emotional upheaval are some examples. The Wicked Witch has sent the monkeys for us. They pick us up, throw us down, tear us apart, and take us to the scary castle. Dang it!

Maybe something is recurring that we experienced before but in a different way. It's giving us another opportunity to make a new, healthier choice and to move toward true, lasting healing. We all get second chances—and more than that—to deal with the monkeys in the world and within each of us. The ego/small self is like the Wicked Witch, thinking that she is separate and grasping for control.

Even the Great and Powerful Oz of our minds doesn't bring the answers or peace that we seek out. Sometimes it takes some help. It took Scarecrow throwing a bucket of water on the Wicked Witch to dissolve her. Fear-based, ego-control... melted.

As awareness of your true spiritual nature rises, your smaller ego self, with its all of struggles and resistance, yields its need to control to the higher self of you. Your truest self is love and well-being, and the captain of your ship.

We're Out of the Woods We're Out of the Dark We're Out of the Night!

We are *all* love and well-being, and we are all connected. You were never alone. You aren't alone now, and you never will be alone.

It just took the beautiful Glinda the Good Witch of the South to remind Dorothy who she was and that she had what she was looking for with her the whole time. She just had to click those ruby slippers together and remember that *she* was her way home. Maybe she had to knock off the mud of misperceptions and struggle that were covering them to be fully free.

In the end, Dorothy was never really lost or alone at all. She was guided along the way to Oz and back—back home to wholeness and connection ... and so are the rest of us.

Wow, there were a lot of twists in this part of the maze. I hope you're still with me! Rest for a little. When you're ready, turn this way...

Musical Offering

"Get Back Up" by TobyMac
"You're Not Alone" by Marie Miller
"Suitcases" by Dara Maclean
"Press On" by Building 429
No Man Is an Island—by Tenth Avenue North

Pearl

You are never alone.

CHAPTER 3

Let's Realize Who We Are

I forgive myself for forgetting that I am divine.
— John-Roger

As Handel's *Messiah* beautifully resounds, we, like the sheep, have all gone astray. The biblical origin of this is found in Isaiah 53:6. Or as a reference to the last chapter's Wizard of Oz analogy, we have fallen asleep in the poppy fields of life. We have forgotten who we really are.

We are an individual expression of the energy of God/Source in physical form. Our true nature is love and well-being. When we lack awareness of this, we perpetuate limits, negative beliefs, and separateness. A mindset of separateness promotes judgement, competition, jealousy, anger, fear, and low self-worth. These negative energies can lead us to withdraw or retaliate in one form or another. A negative, separate mindset promotes a negative, separate outcome, which is not good.

Your True Identity

As Anita Moorjani points out in her great book *Dying To Be Me*[9] (an account of her near-death experience and awakening to love), we are all connected, and we are all one. Problems and struggle arise when we view ourselves and others as disconnected and separate.

> We've created so much judgement about what's "perfect", which leads to doubt and

competitiveness. Since we feel as though we are not good enough, we go around acting out. However, if each of us became aware of our magnificence and felt good about ourselves, it seems to me that the only thing we'd have to share is our unique nature, expressed outwardly in a loving manner that reflects our self-care.

Anita goes on to share that the key to her healing of stage IV cancer—just like all of our healing—is unconditional self-love that eliminates fear and all of its effects. She also writes:

Because most people don't live in the clarity of self-awareness, laws, judgement, rewards, and punishments are required to keep folks from harming each other. If everyone were aware of their own magnificence, then we'd no longer be driven by fear. We wouldn't need rules and jails… and hospitals…

Our manifest world would change to reflect the new state. People would be more self-empowered and far less fearful and competitive, which would lead to more tolerance of each other. Crime rates would drop dramatically. Our immune systems would be stronger from less stress and fear, so there would be fewer illnesses. Priorities would change and we would no longer be driven by greed, which is another facet of fear. Children would grow up being love—being stronger, healthier, and more trusting.

We are each, at the core, a spiritual, infinite being. We have instincts, intuition, and divine inspiration. But in our busy and complicated lives, we lose track of our true inner natures. We react to and identify with other people in our lives, our circumstances, our cultures, our ethnicities, and societal norms. We lose touch with and can't hear our own instinctive spiritual self in the noise of our minds and of the world.

When Anita's spirit ultimately returned to her stage IV lymphoma-ravaged body, she was able to heal and share the truths she learned in her experience. She came to understand that her own fears, judgements, lack of self-love, and disconnection from her true identity as unconditional love promoted her physical cancer. When she returned back to her physical body with the healing realization of who she truly was, her body then healed.

Our physical bodies are made of energy, and they respond to our level of conscious awareness of our true being, which is love. You are love. I am love. We are love… universal, unconditional love.

We are each an individual, yet we are each a connected expression of one love. It is unhindered self-love, expressing its own unique beauty, which is the miracle for all forms of problems and disease. The energy of love is healing. Seeing and respecting the inherit goodness in ourselves and others is oneness.

I'm not referring to an arrogant or narcissistic form of self-love. These are actually fear-based attitudes that reflect a low self-esteem. I'm referring to standing in your own shoes of love and truth.

Self-Criticism or Self-Love?

As we move along in our lives, we can be influenced in many ways to adopt conscious or even unconscious self-criticism. We absorb and internalize the judgements of others. We can be punished for not measuring up to someone's ideals. We are told in one form or another that we aren't quite right. We may be too fat, too thin, the wrong race, from the wrong culture, not smart enough, not attractive enough, the wrong religion, too tall, too short, or have the wrong color hair. The list is long. Unfortunately, the list also changes. What is right and accepted today may be wrong next year or even a few months from now. Who can keep up? Who's doing the deciding and the judging anyway? Sadly, we are. We all are. The saddest is when we judge ourselves. When we negatively judge ourselves, we are not loving ourselves.

Louise Hay, author and founder of Hay House Publishing, offers a list of ways that we don't love ourselves in her book *You Can Heal Your Life*[10]:

> We scold and criticize ourselves endlessly. We mistreat our bodies with food, alcohol, and drugs. We choose to believe we are unlovable. We are afraid to charge a decent price for our services. We create illnesses and pain in our bodies. We procrastinate about things that would benefit us. We live in chaos and disorder. We create debt and burdens. We attract lovers and mates who belittle us or abuse us.

When we don't accept and love ourselves, we are denying our inherent goodness and self-worth. We blame ourselves or often someone else for our feelings. We stamp ourselves as not good enough compared to someone else or for not meeting someone else's standards. We let that stamp influence our thoughts, feelings, and actions—our whole lives. It leads to more separation and more loneliness.

The truth is that we are good enough for ourselves. Approve of yourself. We aren't meant to be good enough for someone else or defined by someone else's approval. To each his or her own.

Got it? Let that sink in.

23

Change Will Do You Good

It just takes a willingness and some practice to reset your inner programming and to change the channel of your thought patterns. Remember, you are not your thoughts. You are the spiritual presence who is aware of your thoughts. You can change your thoughts. You can choose thoughts that you prefer—thoughts that are kind and compassionate instead of critical. Change is possible, and I know you can do it.

It's love that heals, and it starts with self-love. I quote a writing from Rev. Lorraine Cohen[11] here:

> Love and accept yourself completely, just as you are. God does. So can You. Love is food for your soul—nourishing your heart and body. Self-love is an essential part in the spiritual journey of awakening and experiencing the richness of life. When you don't love yourself, health, relationships and finances suffer.

When we love and accept ourselves, we stand in our own unique shoes. When we stand in our own truths, we change the way that we interact with others and our whole lives can change for the better.

Here are some ways to love yourself. It's not selfish; it's healthy!

- Treat yourself as you would your best friend.
- Add healthy self-care practices.
- Laugh and have fun.
- Live in your own integrity.
- Surround yourself with kind, supportive people.
- Let go of negativity and negative people.

- Set healthy boundaries.
- Speak up for yourself.
- Focus on the good.
- Remember your truth and be grateful.

That Future You

Another way to love yourself is to consider your future self in the context of the present moment. What decisions and actions are you making now, and how will they affect you in five, ten or even fifteen years?

This motivating exercise was written by Joel Wade PhD,[12] author of *The Virtue of Happiness*. In his *Mastering Happiness* blog titled, "Having Empathy for Our Future Self." Joel writes:

> Vividly imagining how we might feel in the future from our actions today can be a powerful motivator for more effective living. This is true for little things as well as big ones. If we are considering having that second helping or an unhealthy dessert, we're usually focused on the immediate pleasure of the taste, along with the release of dopamine that promises relief from stress. By imagining how we'll feel afterward … we might find that we don't actually feel so good … wishing we had abstained instead. If we are considering engaging in a dangerous behavior—something that might be thrilling in the moment, but could harm us long term—we're usually focused on the thrill. By imagining the potential fallout the next day, and how we might feel after the thrill is gone, we can interrupt something we

might feel awful about later. We usually think of empathy as something we feel for another person, understanding and feeling compassion for their emotions and circumstances. But our future self is also, in effect, another person. How kind are you to the person you're going to be in 20 minutes from now ... two days from now ... a few years from now? Too often when we're in the grips of strong impulses, temptations, or ingrained habits, we aren't thinking of our future self at all. We're just expecting that poor soul will work it out somehow. They're older, they're tough, and it's "not our problem."

Bad habits and the choices we make *do* affect us. But if we stop to consider the possible consequences, we may find the inner strength to be wise and more loving to that person we are becoming.

We could even go a step higher... Let's not use fear and consequences as our motivation for change. Let's use our love and compassion to lead us forward. We are made of love and compassion. It's in there. Love loves. You are your friend. If your best friend made a poor choice, would you criticize and reject that person? I hope not. I hope you could feel empathy for your friend and stand with him or her through a difficult time.

> Do unto others what you would
> have them do to you.
> —Matthew 7:12 (NIV)

In one sense, the other can be your future self. How you treat yourself now affects your future other self. I think Pope Francis said it best when he said, "There is no other." The presence of God is flowing through you, me, and all of us right now. Let's respect that love that we all are because we are all connected. Please identify as who you really are.

Congrats! You made it through the maze of part one. When you are ready, "Healing with Self-Compassion" is this way...

Musical Offering

"Nothing More" by The Alternate Routes
"All About Love" by Steven Curtis Chapman
"The One Thing" by Paul Colman

Pearl

Love yourself as you love others.

PART TWO

Rx

Name ___You___.

Date ___Today___.

Self-Compassion

Refills ___Unlimited___.

S. Balestrino D.O.

You Are Here...

Let's Keep Going!...

CHAPTER 4

Free Your Mind

The greatest revolution in our generation
is that human beings, who by changing
their inner attitudes of their minds, can
change the outer aspects of their lives.
—Marilyn Ferguson

Glad to see you here! So, we've made it through the first part. It wasn't so hard. We understand that life *is*, indeed difficult, but we have some control in how we navigate our canoes. We know that we have a choice in our focus, thoughts, and feelings. We understand who we are. We've made great progress!

Beliefs

So what is behind our thoughts? It's our beliefs. It is our conscious and unconscious beliefs that affect our thoughts. A belief is just a thought you keep returning to.

Our beliefs and patterns of thinking (our attitudes) alter and create our emotions and actions. What are your beliefs about yourself, about others, and about the world? Are they more negative or more positive? I would say most people don't really think about their beliefs, but like most things worth improving, it's good to get to the bottom of things to really make a difference in the outcome. Our beliefs and attitudes develop with us from childhood to adulthood. Luckily, we can change our beliefs. That's good because we actually become what we believe. Here's the cascade:

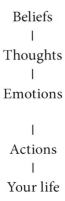

Beliefs
|
Thoughts
|
Emotions

|
Actions
|
Your life

Your beliefs create your thoughts. Your thoughts create your emotions. Your emotions affect your actions. Your actions create your whole life.

Here are some examples of how our beliefs can play out in real life:

- You decide not to try out for the baseball team because you believe you aren't good enough or that you aren't as good as someone else, even though you have a great skill set.
- You choose not to apply for a job opportunity because you feel that you aren't good enough or as qualified as someone else even though you possess the required skills and have a strong desire for the job.
- You don't ask that girl or guy to go out with you because you think you are not worthy of the person's time or affection.

Negativity Is Negative

Is a negative, inferior mindset robbing you of happiness and fulfillment in your life? Have negative experiences created beliefs that are now limiting your choices and actions? Over time, our experiences create our beliefs, and then our beliefs create our experiences. Your future experiences depend on your beliefs. Are they positive and expansive, or are they negative and limiting?

Often, we aren't even aware of our own negative self-talk. We belittle ourselves for not being perfect or measuring up to something or someone else. Sometimes we even curse or blame others for our circumstances and see ourselves as victims. These attitudes and behaviors are harmful and self-defeating.

It can be easy to get stuck there. We get stuck because it seems easier to hang on to what is familiar to us than to hope for something different. Even if what is familiar is uncomfortable or demeaning, we repeat it because it's what we know. As we keep practicing our past experiences, our beliefs are further reinforced. The grooves of our beliefs can run deep.

Some of our inner wounds can also reinforce our beliefs. I get it. You're just trying to protect yourself from more pain. But in your protection, you put up barriers to really healing the wounds and changing your patterns that will help you feel better. You mean well, but you don't realize what you're doing. We can all get in our own ways sometimes.

Emotional wounds, just like physical wounds, need proper care and some time. Picking at the wound doesn't help. Limiting beliefs limit our healing and our lives. To heal, you must be willing to become aware of any patterns of belief, attitudes, and thoughts that are limiting your happiness and personal growth.

You might consider asking yourself the following questions:

- Why do I react that way?
- Why am I self-critical?

- Why am I jealous, judgmental, or critical of others?
- Why don't I try new things?
- Why am I pessimistic?
- What beliefs did I accept that are limiting me now?

What did you come up with? Make some notes. Accept your answers and how you feel. Then, step out of yourself for a moment and see and address yourself as your dear friend. Have some compassion for your friend. You might notice how circumstances led to your current beliefs.

Know that you can challenge your beliefs now and that you can change them.

Choose Anew

Marisa Peer PhD,[13] respected therapist, author, and speaker, tells us that we can change our familiar patterns and choose to create new familiar patterns. You can replace self-criticism, blaming, complaining, and reacting with new beliefs, thoughts, and emotional patterns that support you and feel good. Choose those that you would prefer. Declare them. Speak them out. Marisa reminds us that our minds are listening. Your words are powerful.

You get to choose what beliefs and thought patterns you want to become familiar for you. It just takes practice and repetition. It doesn't even matter if you believe what you are declaring yet or not. Your brain will log your dominant message. Choose wisely and on purpose.

Here are some examples:

- I am good enough.
- I love and accept myself just the way I am.

- I am worthy and valuable.
- I am strong and capable.
- I can focus and accomplish what I put my mind on.
- I'm good at _____.
- I'm a good _____.

Reprogramming is important. Remember the cascade a few pages ago? When we change our beliefs, we can change everything. (Yes, everything.)

Emotions

Your emotions offer valuable guidance. Your emotions give you insight into your current thoughts, thought patterns, mood, and energy level. So, it's important to be aware of how you are feeling. Your emotions are telling you in which direction your energy is going. Are you focused on and moving toward positive, preferred choices, or are you routinely going negative?

Tune in to your own emotional guidance system (EGS). It's very important to check in with yourself on a regular basis and ask, "How am I feeling?" Acknowledge and allow how you feel without judgement or criticism. However you feel is allowed and OK. As respected author and teacher Neal Donald Walsch[14] has said many times, "What you resist, persists." You need to be aware of your feelings to change them.

If you would like to use a printed emotional guidance system, here is one that is often used:

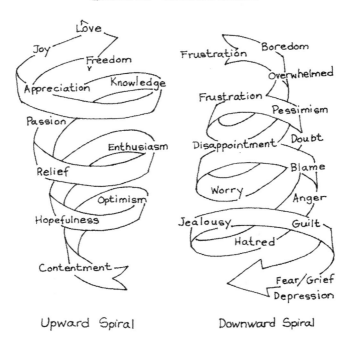

Emotional Guidance Scale

Upward Spiral   Downward Spiral

You can find pictures of these spirals in beautiful colors on the internet.[15] The chart shows both an upward and a downward spiral. You can locate your primary current feeling or where you normally tend to hang out. It's important because, without awareness, our emotional habits can become emotional prisons that promote struggle, negativity, and even contribute to physical illness.

As I mentioned before, feelings can fluctuate even during the course of one day. The goal is to move up the scale as much as you are able in order to achieve relief and feel better. So you can see that your current emotions create your emotional energy level. Your energy levels influence and affect your whole life. It's important. I'll be sharing some ways to change how you feel and move up the scale shortly and even more in chapter 8.

Thoughts

So, what creates our emotions? Our thoughts. What kinds of thoughts are behind your feelings? You may not even be aware that you are thinking because your feelings are so strong (and fast). Usually, there are layers of thoughts that funnel down to the strongest, most basic thought that underlies how you feel.

Here are some examples of both negative and positive feelings and possible thoughts that are behind them:

Negative Feeling	Thoughts Behind the Feeling
Anger	I am not valued. Everyone hurts me.
Hurt	I am unworthy. Nothing will change.
Sad	I am not loved or wanted. It is hopeless.
Lonely	I am not enough. I am a victim.
Fear	I am alone. I can't trust anyone.
Weak	I am powerless. I don't matter.
Positive Feeling	**Thoughts Behind the Feeling**
Hope	I focus on and look for the good.
	I am grateful now and for the future.
Joy and happiness	I am happy just as I am.
	I focus on and look for the good.
Peace	I trust that all is well right now.
Acceptance	I am OK. Life is OK.
Contentment	I am safe.
Love	I love myself as I love others.
	I am worthy and valuable.
Confident	I am capable and powerful.

If you want to change how you feel, you need to change your beliefs and the thoughts that come after them. How do you change them? You uncover and become aware of them, and then you practice changing them.

You need to change the channel of your thoughts to ones that you would prefer. Do you listen to a radio station that you don't really like for very long? It's easy to get stuck on a less desirable channel. We get busy and distracted, and we don't pay enough attention— same channel, same results. But you can physically place your hand above your ear near your head and crank away negative and limiting thoughts by changing your channel. Practice changing your channel to a frequency that feels good and that supports you.

When you find a channel that you like, save it. With practice, you will move your energy and emotions up the scale to an improved mood. Even if you just move up one or two levels, it's still an improvement. Discouragement is still better than anger or rage. Contentment is good. Hopefulness is even better. Our emotional states and levels will fluctuate with the ebb and flow of life. Even nature has rain, snow, and sunshine.

Three Practical Ways to Change

1) Gratitude: Stop, Breathe, and Gratitude (SBG)

The quickest way that I know to improve your emotional state of being is to stop; take three deep, slow breaths; and think of what you are grateful for. Instead of stop, drop, and roll when you're on fire, it's stop, breathe, and gratitude. Use this anytime you are smoldering in the lower levels of the scales. Aren't you sick of smelling smoke?

Start noticing what you *do* have and what is going *right*. Appreciate even the small things that are often taken for granted. Do you have running water, food, and electricity? Do you have clothes and a place to live? Do you have a friend, a family member, a pet, a car, and a phone? Do you *not* have a disease or are you *not* going through a disaster? Or *did* you but came through it?

Were you able to pay your bills? Do you or someone in your family have a job? Did anyone help you?

So when your emotions are in a downward trend, practice gratitude. Gratitude softens and elevates the emotions of anger, fear, frustration, loneliness, and anxiety. Feelings of peace, trust, and love can be restored. Gratitude is healing medicine that has no negative side effects.

SBG anytime you find yourself in a negative mood or circumstance. In fact, develop a morning and evening practice. It will elevate and set the tone for your day and create positive momentum. Gratitude is also a perfect way to enter into restful sleep. Do not review the stress and fatigue of the day and the dread for the next one before you go to sleep. As the beloved Dr. Wayne Dyer tells us in his book *Wishes Fulfilled*, our subconscious minds absorb and use our emotional energetic state even while we sleep to create our lives. Whatever we imprint onto our subconscious minds (day and night, negative and positive) will be copied and created. Our subconscious minds respond to our energetic states. Our subconscious minds, however, don't decide what to print. We control what we put in to our copy machines with our focus of emotion.

Remember, what we focus on gets bigger. Also remember that your emotional focus or mood can be changed. You can change the thoughts and beliefs that fuel your feelings. Gratitude and appreciation are quick and reliable ways to make those changes.

2) Positive personal statements

Write them. Say them. Feel them.

You can call them affirmations, confirmations, or power statements. Just do them. Post them where you can see them. Repeat them. When you acknowledge positive statements about yourself, you are focusing on your strengths and developing your self-love muscles. Mental fitness is important too.

Here are some examples:

- I am strong and confident. I am content. I am peaceful.
- I am energetic and focused. I am kind. I am competent.
- I am healthy. I am a good friend. I am productive. I am forgiving.
- I take good care of myself and others. I am grateful. I am love.
- I am divinely guided. I am enough.

Add some of your own too.

Make your words familiar. Your mind is listening.

3) Let go of negative self-talk and pick up forgiveness

Finally, I encourage you to challenge and delete negative self-talk. Edge out thoughts that promote feelings of guilt, failure, judgement, and unforgiveness. When you hear yourself criticize your imperfections, just stop. Delete it and make a statement that contradicts it. As Marisa Peer suggests, make the self-criticism unfamiliar.

No one gets it all done perfectly. While you're in this human body, you experience a spectrum of choices and abilities. Would you yell at a dear friend for the choices he or she made or didn't make? Would you trash him or her for breaking something or for doing something incorrectly? Would you remind that person of failings throughout his or her life? I hope not. Please don't do it to yourself either.

Step outside of yourself. Let yourself off the hook for moments in time that do not define who you are. Forgiveness cuts the ties of the baggage you are dragging behind you. Imperfection, regret, and unforgiveness are heavy. They use a lot of your energy.

Forgiveness also cuts the ties of attachment to others who hurt you. When you stay focused on past behaviors and hurts, you keep dragging it with you and limiting your energy and your freedom. Accept what is or what was. You don't have to like or condone anything or anyone. Just let it go now. Life gives you feedback for new choices. To drag or not to drag? That is your choice. Love yourself to your freedom. You can do it!

Putting It Together

Remember that you get to choose your beliefs. Positive beliefs promote positive thoughts. Those positive thoughts lead to positive emotions that fuel your choices and actions. People tend to make more positive choices when they feel better. Your sense of well-being improves and so does your whole life experience. Changing and freeing your mind brings healing. Healing is remembering your truth.

Negativity is just a lack of awareness of love. It is a lack of awareness of your true connection and identity. You came from love.

You are love now. You'll be love tomorrow. When you accept that, judgements and insecurities can fall away, and you can feel more peace—"a peace that surpasses all understanding" that Jesus spoke of in the Bible.

When we feel more peaceful, we can use our minds to choose thoughts that are accepting and true. We can experience more positive emotions like hope, joy, optimism, excitement, happiness, and love. We can make choices that promote self-care and growth and that lead to improved relationships and life experiences.

Will life then be easy? No. But when you feel better and change your perspective about yourself and others, your tolerance and resilience to the waves of life improves. When you know who you are, you can see things differently and act differently.

You can choose your beliefs, thoughts, emotions, and actions on purpose. Adopt them and practice them. Make them so familiar that you become a new you. Keep practicing self-love and love for others. It's your realization and realignment with love that is your freedom, your medicine, and your healing.

Pick up your pearl. You're finding your way through. Turn here.

Musical Offering

"Love Alone Is Worth the Fight" by Switchfoot
"Hard Love" by Need To Breathe
"Feel It" by Toby Mac
"Happy" by Pharrell Williams

Pearl

Your beliefs, thoughts, and
feelings create your life.

CHAPTER 5

Self-Love and Compassion Heal

Your task is not to seek for love, but merely
to seek and find all the barriers within
yourself that you have built against it.
—Rumi

Nice work. You made it. So, looking back a bit, I mentioned that it's your remembrance of who you are, your self-love, and your connection to love that is healing. Please read that again.

Now, let's keep moving forward. If the energy of love that you are at your core is not obstructed, resisted, or blocked in some manner, it is fully expressed and supports your well-being.

Healing involves the interconnections of the mind, body, emotions, and spirit. They all affect and reinforce each other. When you make those positive changes in your beliefs and thoughts, you enjoy improved emotions. When you shift how you feel for the better and let go of self-defeating patterns, you flow that improved energy to your body. Your body will have improved energy to use for health, repair, immunity, and well-being. The thoughts you think, your mood, and your feelings are energy in motion to your body. What emotional energy are you bathing your body in? Higher energies and feelings promote your health and well-being.

Emotions and Health

Treating the body must include addressing your mind and your feelings. We physicians can treat the body in all sorts of ways: pills, injections, surgery, chemotherapy, and nutritional and physical therapies. But if your mindset is programmed with guilt, anger, defeat, fear, or depression, your cure will likely be short-lived or not even realized. Negative emotional states can limit your happiness and your health. (No, it's not your fault. I'm here to help you see your truth, help you see that change is possible, and show you how.) Likewise, when you feel happiness and have a more positive mindset, you have enhanced your body's available energy to use as it needs for optimal health.

Traditional medicine has long been taught in a seemingly backward way. We examine, take measurements, run tests, gather data, and look at the *results*. From these *results* we make a diagnosis. Then we go back to the body to target whatever contributed to the *results* by prescribing treatments.

I believe we need to be vigilant to include an assessment for the emotional contributions to a diagnosis and how they affect one's self-care. As an empathic physician, I could feel how my patients felt. I noticed how someone's emotions and mood affected their levels of health and well-being. I noticed that how you feel can affect your blood pressure, your diabetes, and your overall ability to heal. How you feel also affects how well you take care of yourself. Emotions contribute to both disease and well-being. I saw my patients who had a positive mindset thrive and survive cancer. I also saw that when people were depressed, they didn't manage their diabetes well, take their medicines correctly, or do their best to improve their conditions.

That's why it is so important that you become more aware of your beliefs and thoughts. They are creating your feelings, which are affecting your body's health. Your emotional energy is critical to your overall health.

You may be thinking, *But aren't there pills for how you feel?* Yes, there are. They have their place and can be helpful and effective. But it's important to not step over the question of *why* you feel sad, anxious, or depressed. It's important to include and address the root causes of how you feel to most effectively improve your result. To treat the flower with fungicide won't be effective if you haven't treated the soil it's growing in and the roots. (I'm not a plant specialist, but you get what I'm saying, right?) Ineffective or partial treatment gives ineffective or partial results. We must address the body, mind, emotions, and spirit to effectively care for ourselves and each other.

What Can We Do?

So, what can we do to improve our emotional and physical health?

Let's address emotional health first, and I will talk about more traditional physical care and health in the next chapter.

As I mentioned earlier, we all log a myriad of emotional impressions as we grow and interact with our environments. Some impressions are good; some are not. It's the impressions we log as negative that can cause problems. Maybe you received a message that made you feel unloved, rejected, unworthy, sad, or not good enough. These feelings can intensify over time to anger, resentment, bitterness, fear, and other emotions. Emotional messages become emotional impressions that can be expressed and/or stored in varying degrees. We can be aware (conscious) of them or not (unconscious). We may have even falsely interpreted a situation or a message, but we still logged it as an impression.

As you recall, emotions and their impressions can affect your whole life, including your mental and physical health. Everything is connected. The more negative emotional impressions you are able to uncover, the better.

It can take a nudge to expose or see and feel a stored emotional impression. Sometimes it takes an upsetting, repeating pattern of behavior that really shows up to be seen and is clearly calling for attention.

A personal crisis may also shine a light on an old wound. It might be something as simple as a conversation with a trusted friend that exposes an inner truth that is ready to be seen, accepted, let go of, and healed. These moments usually come to be appreciated in hindsight. You may think, *Yes, that was bad, but I get it now.* Everyone is different, and so are our struggles and stories. It makes sense that we will also differ in the process and timing of our healings and growth.

Luckily, there are also many different ways to change or heal emotional impressions. You need only to be open and willing to explore different methods. You can choose what feels right for you.

If you don't like one method, try a different one. It is often useful to use a number of techniques and tools to release old impressions that are limiting you and to create new, healthier impressions.

No matter what you choose, I suggest that you bring acceptance, forgiveness, kindness, patience, and love for yourself. Remember that best friend of yours? That person deserves your care and kindness.

Dr. Sheila Balestrino

Healing emotional impressions requires a level of acceptance of what *was* and of what *is*. Think: *It happened... It affected me... I see it...*

It's also important to understand that the people who were involved in creating your impressions and circumstances were acting from *their* level of awareness (or lack of it) at that time. Imperfect people affect the imperfect people around them.

Sometimes it's helpful to recall a scenario that affected you as if you were an outside observer. This can lessen the intensity of your feelings a bit.

Acceptance, compassion, and forgiveness are essential elements that are weaved through the many techniques you may use to release and heal limiting impressions.

Here is a list of some of the tools, practices, and resources that can promote improvement and healing of emotional impressions:

- Prayer. In its many forms, prayer is communicating with your God, Source, or Higher Power. Often prayer involves offering gratitude and our heartfelt intentions.
- Meditation. There are many forms of meditation. It's a practice of quieting the mind to connect with spirit in stillness, with more of a listening and receiving intent.
- Mindfulness. Mindfulness is just practicing present-moment awareness.
- Traditional therapists, counselors, and coaches.
- Rapid transformational therapy (RTT). This is Marisa Peer's combination work that includes hypnotherapy.
- Spiritual or religious support systems, teachers, and community.

- Energy therapies and medicine. These include Reiki, Quantum-Touch, Eden Method, chakra work, and the Emotional Freedom Technique (EFT) or tapping.
- Yoga, tai chi, and qigong. These unite the breath, body, mind, and spirit through exercise and postures that promote healthy energy, flow, relaxation, and well-being.
- Compassion Key. Keep reading for more information.

All of these, and more, can address, promote, and restore emotional balance and well-being. Choose what you prefer.

What Is Compassion Key?

I think I always had a desire to help people to feel better. When others felt better, I would feel better. So I went to nursing school, became an RN, and then went to medical school. I have been a board-certified family medicine physician for more than thirty years now.

In the last decade, I also became certified as a coach and a Compassion Key practitioner. The coaching program helped me integrate nontraditional understandings of emotional energy and how it impacts and creates our lives. Compassion Key helped me more deeply understand how emotional healing can occur and how it can not only transform how you feel but also transform your whole life.

Compassion Key[16] is a very effective way to heal emotional issues, impressions, and experiences that are affecting and limiting your life, regardless of whether you are aware of them. Compassion Key can heal impressions or negative feelings, and it works at the root level. Some examples would be a feeling or experience of being unworthy, abandoned, betrayed, abused, mistreated, neglected, unloved, alone, unseen, weak, forgotten, broken, or damaged.

Letting go of these emotional impressions is healing. It's like shaking off the layers of dirt or mud that you have accumulated throughout your life to reveal the real soul of you that has been there all along. Picture a light trying to shine through a lens with dirt or mud on it. The picture, which represents your life, would be distorted. When you remove the dirt and mud, the full light of your soul can shine through. You are free to create a happier life.

We can release those emotional impressions that we carry with us through our lives. The truth is, we can't just think and label our emotional impressions away. When we meet them with love and compassion, we can release and heal them. We can then experience relief and feel better. Then we can make new and better choices in all areas of our lives. When we release emotional patterns of pain and struggle, we stop creating more of the same.

Because my work is rooted in love and compassion, I have integrated the tool of Compassion Key. I teach and offer Compassion Key in my course ReNew Your Life Now! And I also offer private sessions. You can find out about me and the course at my website. You can find my email there also to message me with any questions or to book a session.

DrSheilaBalestrino.com[17]
info@drsheilabalestrino.com

Compassion Key involves sending healing love and compassion inward to yourself for whatever negative feeling or issue that is present in your life. What you meet with compassion dissolves.

There is a short form and a long form of Compassion Key. You can learn and use the short form yourself, while the long form is usually guided by a practitioner or support person.

I'll describe the short form for you here. Whenever you are aware of a negative feeling, take a moment to tune in and get clear on the emotion. For example, are you feeling anger, fear, sadness, grief, insult, or shame? Once you are clear on the feeling, notice where you feel it in your body. Take a few slow, deep breaths to calm your nervous system and settle in your heart area. Then you can begin sending compassion inward to yourself for whatever you are experiencing, whether it be a feeling, a judgement of yourself or others, or a circumstance. You send phrases inward to yourself that begin: "I'm so sorry that you..." You complete the sentence with words that describe how you feel and things that occurred that upset you. You use your own words in any way that is real for you. No one is listening. This is for *you*.

Following are a few examples:

Feelings

- I'm so sorry that you feel lonely.
- I'm so sorry that you feel embarrassed.

Situations

- I'm so sorry you lost your job.
- I'm so sorry you have to work with her.

Judgements

- I'm so sorry things never work out for you.
- I'm so sorry you aren't good enough.

You say *you* because you are speaking to yourself and sending your compassion within. When you feel you have expressed yourself and that you are complete, you can then add some phrases that remind you who you are and to lock it in. These phrases begin: "And now you can remember…"

For example:

- And now you can remember that you are never alone.
- And now you can remember that your value comes from within.
- And now you can remember that you are powerful.
- And now you can remember that you are OK just as you are and that no one controls how you feel.
- And now you can remember that you are your source of your well-being.
- And now you can remember that you are and have always been enough.

Phrases to add:

- I love you just the way you are.
- I choose to see things differently.
- I choose to be different.
- I choose healing now.
- And now I am free.

You can place your hand over the area in your body where you felt your initial emotion and breathe in love and healing compassion there.

Say to yourself: "I accept this healing of my body, mind, and spirit … Thank you!"

The healing energy of compassion dissolves and releases our emotional impressions. It addresses impressions that we are aware of and those we may not even be consciously aware of but are logged in the subconscious.

Sometimes, when you are guided in a Compassion Key session, phrases may seem to not make sense for you, or they may even sound harsh. We are not necessarily validating the phrase as true, but we are covering and releasing *all* impressions related to your area of focus.

We accumulate many stored memories or impressions as we grow through infancy, childhood, and into adult life. Emotions and experiences stick to us. When you release emotional impressions or emotions in the moment, you feel relief right away. You will also notice that you just feel better in general. When you feel better, you make healthier choices and your life can improve in all areas. You can feel better about yourself, be more confident, improve your relationships, be more productive at work or home, be less stressed, become healthier, improve your finances, and even release addictions and unhealthy habits.

Compassion Key involves the heart, mind, and soul, and it always works. It works at the root level where it is most effective.

But keep in mind that you can't fully heal an impression while hanging on to its perceived benefit—for example, playing the victim or hanging on to anger to protect yourself will limit your healing.

You need to be willing to let go of what is holding you back with love and acceptance. Love and acceptance are in that secret sauce of gratitude. Together, they are healing magic. Compassion Key can help you to raise your *life set-point*—the point from which you create your life ... for the better!

When you learn to manage your emotional energy more easily, you make great strides forward through life's twists and turns. Life is more manageable. Your improved energy flows to and bathes your body. Your body thanks you and supports you with improved health.

Speaking of the body, the next chapter will review the many ways you can take care of your physical body—the easy part. Well, maybe not, but it's probably more familiar.

Follow me this way...

Musical Offering

"Where the Light Shines
Through" by Switchfoot
"Stand By You" by Rachel Platten
"Whole Heart" by Brandon Heath
"Love Never Fails" by Brandon Heath
"Power of Love" by Luther Vandross

Pearl

Your love and compassion heals.

CHAPTER 6

The Body

If only one thing is healed in your life, it should
be the separation between mind and body.
— Deepak Chopra and Rudolph
E. Tanzi, *The Healing Self*[18]

OK, great! You made it. Maybe the body doesn't sound easy, but at least we have a lot of data on what promotes health and healing—if you like data, that is. It's kind of a long trail, but it's important. I have chosen to highlight six topics. Come on, let's keep moving...

Mind-Body

We talked about your mind and how your emotional energy impacts your physical body. After all, your physical body *is* energy. From the smallest molecule to the largest organs in the body, each cell is made of energy and affects neighboring cells. You are a collection of vibrational energy in physical form.

There are *plenty* of books and resources that address the mind-body and spirit connection. One of them is the latest edition of *The Biology of Belief* by Bruce Lipton, Ph.D. In this book, he describes how brain cells coordinate neurochemical signals to the cells of the entire body. These neurochemicals influence genetic and behavioral activity. Your conscious and subconscious beliefs set forth a chain of neurochemical events that affect your biology—your body. Your beliefs, thoughts, and emotional energy are integral parts of your body's environment. Your overall health is a combination of your genetic disposition, your beliefs and inner state of being, your outer environment, and your personal habits and lifestyle.

Dr. Lipton has spoken and written in great detail on the field of epigenetics. Epigenetics refers to how our genes are influenced and affected by our environments and experiences. Are you bathing in and sending out neurochemical habits of lower, fear-based energies such as anxiety, resentment, or depression? Or are you sending higher energies and neurochemicals that are based in love like peace, contentment, acceptance, and happiness? You have a choice, and your energy will influence your overall health. Dr. Lipton writes:

> This research has confirmed that brain cells translate the mind's perceptions (beliefs) of the world into complementary and unique chemical profiles that, when secreted into the blood, control the fate of the body's 50 trillion cells. So blood, the body's culture medium, not only nourishes cells, it's neurochemical components also regulate cells' genetic and behavioral activity... When we change the way we perceive the word, that is, when we "change our beliefs" we change the blood's neurochemical composition, which then initiates a complimentary change in the body's cells. The function of the mind is to create coherence between our beliefs and the reality we experience.[19]

So, the cells of your body will receive the neurochemicals that your mind and emotions are sending. Lower, more negative emotions and stress promote inflammation, inhibit immune function, and can promote disease. Stress has even been shown to reduce the length of telomeres, which are end caps of certain DNA; this correlates with a shortened longevity. Inflammation is known to be a key contributor to many devastating medical conditions. These include cardiovascular diseases, diabetes, Alzheimer's disease, and cancer.

Positive emotions and outlooks, on the other hand, promote a healthy immune system, improve states of well-being, and preserve telomere length. Happiness really *is* the best medicine. And the energy of love, in its many forms, is as important as nutrition and even our genetics.

Deepak Copra and Rudolph Tanzi also state in their book, *The Healing Self,* that "Reality goes where belief leads."[20]

Your body is part of your reality and environment. It's important to actively counter any negative or unhealthy beliefs with more positive, health-promoting beliefs. It's not hard, and, in fact, it's *vital* to your health. It just takes *practice* and *repetition*. It takes your will to change for the better. You are the master of your beliefs, your mind, and the energy that you flow to your body.

Nutrition

On to nutrition... Nutrition and diet are very broad topics that span extensive amounts of literature. I will highlight and condense current information (as of the time of this writing) that I think is important. This will not be comprehensive. You can search these resources and more as you like.

The healthiest diets are rich in nutrients and fiber (prebiotics) and contain healthy fats. A healthy diet avoids processed junk foods, unhealthy fats, and most sugar, white flour, and gluten-containing items. This way of eating, in calorie moderation, also promotes optimal health and weight management. Obesity promotes negative health conditions and diseases. It is also best to limit red meats, which can also lead to many health conditions and diseases.

The Mediterranean diet[21] gets consistently high ratings as a healthy diet. This is in part due to the longer life expectancy in people who live in Mediterranean areas. This diet reduces the risks of diabetes, heart disease, and certain cancers. It also is better for the environment in many ways.

The Mediterranean diet limits red meat and processed foods and includes an array of fresh produce and whole grains. Fatty fish like salmon or tuna, olive oil, avocado, nuts, and seeds provide the healthy or unsaturated fats. My daughter Lisa, a registered dietician with a master of science degree, says:

> In contrast to the healthy fats, unhealthy fats, also called saturated or trans fats, are the form of fat often found in animal products and highly processed foods. Foods high in saturated fats include marbled (fatty) meat, processed breakfast meats like bacon or sausage, whole milk and butter. A healthy diet contains less than 7% of your daily calories as saturated fat. Trans fats are found in stick margarine, shortening, some fried foods, baked goods, and packaged foods made with partially hydrogenated oils. It is recommended to avoid intake of trans fats when you can.[22]

Another area of focus that has emerged is an anti-inflammatory diet.[23] Just as stress can promote inflammation in the body, certain foods can also promote inflammation. Inflammatory foods contain sugar, saturated fats, and gluten, and are often processed and fried.

Examples are: Mayonnaise, grain-fed meats, farm-raised fish, sodas, pastries, margarine, many salad dressings, and processed baked goods, and crackers. Avoid soybean and canola oils.

Here are some anti-inflammatory foods to include in your diet:

- avocado oil, olive oil, and coconut oil
- walnuts, Brazil nuts, pecans, cashews, and almonds
- grass-fed red meats and dairy
- wild cold-water fish with omega 3 fatty acids, such as salmon, tuna, trout, sardine, anchovy, mackerel, and herring
- fruits, such as berries, cherries, pineapple, papaya, apples, and grapes (and their red wine)
- leafy greens and cruciferous vegetables
- tomatoes, asparagus, and mushrooms
- spices and herbs, including ginger, basil, thyme, garlic, clove, turmeric, and cinnamon
- green tea and dark chocolate/cocoa

Got it? OK.

Now let's mention superfoods. Superfood lists,[24] like many recommendations, can vary. Superfoods are said to promote health and longevity and are rich in antioxidants, which protect your cells from free radicals that form when you break down foods or are exposed to toxins.[25] Free radicals can damage cells and cause illness and aging.

Here are some of the antioxidants that are found in superfoods:[26]

- vitamins C and E
- glutathione
- CoQ10
- alpha-lipoic acid

- astaxanthins
- flavonoids
- resveratrol

Many of the anti-inflammatory foods overlap with the long list of superfoods. Here are some of the superfoods:

- broccoli
- spinach
- sweet potatoes
- salmon
- avocado
- greens and kale
- blueberries
- flaxseed
- nuts
- green tea
- coffee
- dark chocolate,
- apples
- olive and coconut oil
- mushrooms
- asparagus

All of these foods can promote health and resist disease states. In addition, specific cancer-fighting or -resisting foods have been identified. In his book, *The 31-Day Food Revolution*, Ocean Robbins[27] sites data to support these benefits in mushrooms, cruciferous vegetables, and celery. Also, the company GreenMedInfo[28] adds evidence to support these benefits in green tea, caffeine, turmeric, and curcumin. This site also has noteworthy information on the genesis of cancer cells. An e-book titled *GreenMedInfo's Top 6 Evidence-based Cancer Fighting Foods* is available for download on their website: GreenMedIinfo.com.

I do understand that there is a lot of diet information available, and there are many types of diets. Diets come and go, and the changes can be confusing and frustrating. I am not going to describe all of them, but I will mention a few here. You may have heard of the Paleo diet, which avoids dairy, sugar, and grains but includes meats. A vegan diet is plant-based and also avoids dairy. Both ways of eating have some health pros and cons. That is likely why Dr. Mark Hyman, a functional medicine physician at the Cleveland Clinic, wrote the book *The Pegan Diet*.[29] This diet combines the best principles of the vegan and Paleo diets, while keeping in mind our individuality with food as our own unique medicine.

Also, it's not a diet, but if you are interested in the health benefits of intermittent fasting, I would consider reading the book *Fast This Way* by Dave Asprey.[30] He is the founder of Bulletproof Coffee and is a rock star of biohacking for health and longevity.

Whatever diet you live (and eat) by, try to stay within healthy guidelines. Did you notice the overlap and repetition of some of the health-promoting foods? Try to include them in your diet. *Do* try the best that you can, because when your body is healthy, your body and mind function better and you feel better. Nutrition is medicine.

Finally, *do* wash all of your nutrition down with plenty (six eight-ounce servings) of clean, filtered water and not chemical-rich soda.

Gut Health

Volumes of information is available about gastrointestinal health as well. It's true that we *are* what we eat ... and what we absorb ... and a collection of microbes called a microbiome.

Yes, that gut microbiome you hear about is important. We are each a microbiome. A microbiome is a collection of microorganisms that are essential and beneficial in our development, protection, immunity, and nutrition.[31] We are actually composed of more microbes than cells. OK, now let that thought go.

The microbiome varies from person to person and culture to culture. In general, prebiotic fiber is good for gut bacteria and helps reduce inflammation. Too much inflammation can lead to what is called leaky gut, which occurs when the good versus bad bacteria in the gut are out of ideal balance. This can happen as a result of a diet rich in sugars, processed foods, alcohol, and even stress. In this environment, the intestinal lining that controls what is absorbed back into the body, doesn't work as well. As a result, undigested foods, toxins, and microbes leak back into the bloodstream This has been linked to irritable bowel syndrome and many autoimmune diseases.[32]

So, to reduce gastrointestinal issues, it is best to remove foods that are inflammatory and include anti-inflammatory foods and supplements. Also, limit or remove alcohol consumption and work at managing and reducing stress.

You can add prebiotic fiber in your diet with fiber-rich foods or fiber supplements. You can also consider including good microbes in the form of a probiotic supplement or the routine addition of yogurt or fermented or pickled foods in your diet.

Finally, you can consider getting your gut health tested. One company that does this is called Viome.[33] Your results will give you specific information on best foods for *your* gut and what foods to eat less of or to avoid.

Exercise

Movement is good for your body, so find ways to move that you don't dislike and do them on a fairly regular basis. Exercise will not only help to manage your weight and help prevent health conditions and diseases but will also help you feel better emotionally and physically, as well as aid in improved sleep patterns.

Exercise can assist with the cessation of tobacco and other unhealthy habits. Exercise and other techniques and activities increase endorphins in the body, which promote a feeling of well-being and reduced pain perception.[34]

Exercise promotes brain, cardiovascular, muscle, bone, and sexual health as we age. It can also help reduce your risk for injury or falls. Exercise helps to reduce stress, and it's inflammatory effects. Exercise is medicine, as it can promote a healthier and longer life.[35]

How much, and how often? It varies by your age, ability, and goals. If you are inactive or if you have medical conditions that limit you, it's best to start slower and check in with your local health professional before you start.

For adults, recommendations aim for about 150 minutes of moderate-intensity or 75 minutes of vigorous-intensity aerobic physical activity per week... or a combination of the two types. Strengthening activities should be included at least twice a week, which may include exercise bands, weights, sit-ups, and push-ups. Try to include all muscle groups for your arms, core, and legs.

For children and teens, Recommendations are for sixty minutes or more of physical activity every day. Look for age-and skill-appropriate fun, such as playing games. Hopping, skipping, and jumping is exercise. Teens can begin to lift weights.[36]

If you have a goal to lose weight, you may need to exercise more and increase your physical activity while watching what and how much you eat. Sometimes, things *do* make sense.

Try different activities. Walking counts. Just make a decision to be active and put the time in for your health and well-being. You will feel better!

Sleep

Get some! Getting adequate sleep is as important as nutrition and exercise. Sleep allows your body and mind to recharge and prevent diseases. Inadequate sleep reduces mental clarity and immune function and can promote cardiovascular disease and diabetes. Poor sleep has also been linked to depression and to inflammation in the body.

Seven to nine hours per day is recommended for an adult.[37] Some people seem to require less, but it is important. Personal sleep patterns vary, and there is no right or wrong.

> There is no morality in waking up early or staying up late. There is a huge amount of power in finding out when you sleep best and then building your life so that you can sleep.[38]

This is a quote from Dave Asprey's book *Game Changers*, in which he offers best strategies for the human experience in health, happiness, and success. In this book, he interviewed Dr. Michael Breus,[39] a well-known clinical psychologist and sleep expert. Dr. Breus has described four types of circadian rhythm-based sleep types, and he named them each after a mammal of the same sleep type. He describes the sleep patterns of the bear, lion, wolf, and dolphin.

- Bear: About 50 percent of people are bears. Their awake-sleep patterns follow the sun. They don't have sleep problems.
- Lion: These are the early birds who are busy in the mornings and tend to wind down in the evening. About 15 percent of people follow this pattern.
- Wolf: These are the night owls who are most productive in the afternoon and the late evening. About 15 percent of people are wolves.
- Dolphin: These are the light sleepers who tend to have interrupted sleep, usually because of their thoughts.

There is a site that you can take a quiz to find out your type if you wish: www.thepowerofwhenquiz.com. You can also just take some time off and notice your own natural pattern. I know that work, schedules, kids, and family responsibilities can take and keep you off of your natural circadian rhythm. When possible, try to shift your life responsibilities to better fit your own natural sleep rhythm. It makes sense, it's interesting, and it's kind of fun, right?

In addition, to guard your sleep, please discipline yourself about watching television and staying up too late. It's best to avoid computer and cell phone screens close to bedtime. Also, try to keep your bedroom dark.

Asprey adds that it's important to go outside during the day to expose yourself to natural sunlight. The serotonin that this produces breaks down to melatonin, which helps you sleep at night.

Finally, if you have sleep apnea, seek medical guidance for treatment options that are right for you.

Do your best to get your sleep because, as it turns out, sleep is medicine too.

Harmful—Helpful

I'll start with the harmful. Please avoid tobacco products and excessive use of alcohol. These toxins have a long list of known health consequences. Actually, do your best to avoid *all* toxic chemical exposures and pollutants in your environment, including in the products you use and in the food and drink you consume. It all adds up, and it does matter.

Toxins and chemicals have been shown to contribute to cognitive decline, autoimmune diseases, cardiovascular diseases, diabetes, and cancers.[40] Here are some of the known toxins:

- BPA (bisphenol A): found in plastic and canned foods and drinks
- aluminum: found in the air, soil, food, foil, pans, water, and deodorants
- mercury: found in some fish
- pesticides: found in food, water, and some disinfectants
- oxybenzone and parabens: found in some cosmetics
- phthalates: found in plastics
- PAHs (polycyclic aromatic hydrocarbons): found in grilled or smoked red meats
- trans fats and sugars

Harmful items can be inflammatory themselves, contribute to inflammation, or both. One system in your body affects another.

As mentioned earlier, even stress creates inflammation. A minor stress, such as a cut on a finger, produces an appropriate cortisol stress response to heal. Chronic, unmanaged stress, on the other hand, sends the fight-or-flight cortisol response into overdrive, leading to fatigue and compromised health.

On the helpful side, do your best to learn ways to manage your stress levels because life includes stress. Many of these were mentioned in the last chapter. Support and forgive yourself. Keep a few trusted friends, and don't let the rest ruffle you. You be you and let them be them. Trying to be or please someone else is tiring and only creates more stress.

It's best to be in healthy contact with others. Isolation isn't healthy for the body, mind, or spirit; however, too much social-media time doesn't promote peace either. Unplug from the noise and set limits. Go outside (with that sunscreen on) and clear the air of your mind. Tune in to the music of the birds.

Remember that gratitude is the secret sauce that brings clarity and peace. Look at and focus on what you *do* have and what is going *right* in your life. Smile and find things that make you laugh. Sometimes you just have to laugh at yourself!

Eat, drink, move, and sleep healthy. Cultivate and nourish a healthy self-awareness and appreciate your value. See the value of others and your connection to everyone and everything.

That was a condensed version of some of the main healthy-body-promoting information. Resources are at the end of the book under this chapter (six). I hope you will strive to begin and/or continue these healthy practices of self-care for the magnificent body you are living in.

As you can see, everything is connected in a vibrant balance of body, mind, and spirit. Each requires, supports, and nourishes the other. If you neglect one, the whole suffers. If you love each one, the whole flourishes.

Great job! We've covered a lot of ground in this maze of life so far. You've made it through self-awareness and self-care. Maybe you want to grab some water and rest. The last section is around the bend. I'll meet you there when you're ready. You've got this!

Musical Offering

"It's Your Life" by Francesca Battistelli
"Love Take Me Over" by Steven Curtis Chapman

Pearl

Your health is a combination of your
genetic disposition, your beliefs,
your outer environment, and your
personal habits and lifestyle.

PART THREE

Rx

Name _____ *You* _____ .

Date __ *Today* __ .

Self-Care

Refills __ *Every day* __ .

S. Balestrino D.O.

You Are Here...

Almost There!

CHAPTER 7

Create Anew!

> Once you believe in yourself and see yourself
> as divine and precious, you'll automatically be
> converted to a being who can create miracles.
> —Dr. Wayne Dyer

So happy to see you here! You made it through to this last section, and I'm so proud of your perseverance. Perseverance is required to make new changes for the better.

In this chapter, I'm going to lead you through a process that will help you to become clearer on what you are wanting in all areas of your life. This process is called clarity through contrast. I became aware of this tool in my coaching program.[41] I also use this process in my course ReNew Your Life Now!, which is detailed on my webpage: DrSheilaBalestrino.com.

To create something new, you first need to become very clear on what you would prefer in all areas of your life, including:

- career/work
- physical health
- relationships
- finances
- personal habits or addictions
- self-confidence and self-love
- spiritual growth/life

You are the creator of the rest of your life's story. How do you want it to be? Remember that your very beliefs and thoughts are creating your life, so *choose* them on purpose. Let's rewire and reprogram outdated and less-than-happy-and-healthy data for new and better data. You just need to get clear on what better looks and feels like to *you*. Everyone's perspective is a bit different.

This is simple. It just may take a few minutes, and that's OK. You and your life are worth it. First, take out a sheet of paper and then draw a long vertical line down the middle. Write "Don't Want" as the heading on the left side and "Do Want" as the heading on the right.

Let's start with the life area of career/work. You can write that on the top if you like. Starting on the left side, list all of the types, ways, conditions, and particulars that you do *not* want in a work experience. Be very specific. Here is an example:

Career/Work

Don't Want   Do Want

I don't want a desk job.
I don't want to swing shifts.
I don't want to have to travel.
I don't want to commute more than thirty minutes.
I don't want to work manual labor.
I don't want to make less than: ____.
I don't want to work in a big city.
I don't want to work alone.
I don't want to work more than __ hours per week.

When you have completed this side of the paper, you will now have a reference to more clearly focus on what you *do want* and what you would prefer in your work/career. Now make a contrasting statement of wherever, whenever, and however you would prefer to work on the right side of the paper. This can also work for a stay-at-home parent. Be very specific and take a moment to ask yourself: "Why do I want this?" and "How will this make me feel?"

In the end, it's about how we *feel* that matters. What work preferences will help you to feel less stressed, appreciated, happy, productive, and fulfilled? You can also list, "How I will feel," at the bottom of the page.

Here are some examples for the Do Want list:

Don't Want   Do Want

                      I want to move around at work.
                      I want to work from 8 or 9 a.m. to 4 or 5 p.m.
                      I want a set location.
                      I want to live less than thirty minutes from work.
                      I want an office or clerical job.
                      I want to make $____.
                      I want to work in a smaller town.
                      I want to work with others.
                      I prefer to work ____ hours per week.

How I will feel: _____

_____.

Your Do Want list and your feelings are what you will focus on. What you *focus* on gets *bigger.* Now, please repeat this process for all of the life areas. It won't take long, and it's worth your time. When you are finished, you will have your *own personal* life preferences to focus on, to feel, and to pull you forward. Things don't start to move until we think, see, feel, and talk about where we are going.

In between where you are *now* and where you would *prefer* to be is that buffer of time area. It calls for us to stand in the fertile soil of contentment, appreciation, gratitude, peace, and confidence. Change your mental channels to the higher energy frequencies. Believe that what you want is on the way. As Dr. Wayne Dyer has said: "You have to believe it before you see it."

When you place an order with Amazon, do you believe that it will come? Almost 100 percent, right? I picture my list of desires as having been received by the universal warehouse. It's up there. It's coming. This helps me generate the good-feeling energy (secret sauce) that is needed. I smile and just keep checking the metaphorical porch. Is it here yet? What does it look like? Not yet? OK. I keep smiling, knowing that it's still coming. I have learned to trust universal timing; they know what they're doing.

Here's what you *do* with your Do Want lists. In the morning when you are getting ready for your day, review, feel, and even visualize your preferred scenario for all areas of your life. Make sure you *feel* the good feelings that go with them. You can thank God/the Universe for bringing them to you and add, "This or something better!"

Try not to muddy the good-feeling waters with worry and fear by trying to figure out the details of how or when you will see what you are focusing on. This can short-circuit and interrupt or even block your results. Hold each thought and feeling for about twenty to thirty seconds, smile, and when you are done, move on with your day. Do this again in the evening or before bed.

Repetition is important to keep your focus, to reprogram your thoughts, and to elevating your energy for success. Your mind is listening to your thoughts and feelings. You get back the energy you are sending out. Your outcomes will match your beliefs. Repeat the positive beliefs.

Negative thought patterns cultivate lower energies and tend to produce more negative results. A more positive mindset, on the other hand, tends to produce higher energies and a more positive trail of results. It is important to believe in yourself and your desires. It is also important to do your best to feel content right where you are now, as you look forward to the good that is coming. Because it's the *now* feelings that are creating your day and your tomorrows. Yikes! Check in with yourself often. What are you thinking and feeling? What would you prefer? Do you need to make an adjustment? Do you need to hop on the gratitude train?

The good news is that just as your mind is listening, so is your soul/God/the Universe. What you call your life is really a cocreation, so to speak. You are never alone. But you get to choose. Maybe things will turn out differently and take more time than you imagined or thought. OK. Life is a process of becoming more aware of what your inner spiritual self was trying to do, be, and create all along. It's a process that includes change, which is a natural part of life.

If you want to change and improve any area of your life, it takes an *awareness*, a *desire*, a *will*, and a *commitment*. It's not that tall of an order. Just like anything that is worth an effort, it will take practice and repetition. Practice and repeat more positive thoughts, feelings, and actions, and you will create the changes you want to see in your life.

In the next chapter, you're going to bring your Do Want lists and feelings, along with your new awareness and understandings, to create your own *personal plan* to feeling better! And when you feel better, your life improves for the better. I lovingly refer to your plan as your Daily Disciplines. These are disciplines of healthy habits and self-care that keep you feeling better from one day to the next ... and the next. This is how you renew your life.

Take time to review your lists and feel the good feelings. Practice putting this time in your day.

When you are ready, walk with me. We are close to putting all of these pieces together and finding our way out of this maze called life. This way ...

Musical Offering

"Shining Star" by Earth, Wind & Fire
"Live Out Loud" by Steven Curtis Chapman
"Life in My Day" by NewSong
"Do Life Big" by Jamie Grace

Pearl

You are the creator of your life's story.

CHAPTER 8

Daily Disciplines

A river cuts through rock, not because of
its power, but because of its persistence.
—Jim N. Watkins

Prep Talk

Hi there, new you in progress! I hope you have already started to focus on those things, conditions, and outcomes that you would prefer in all areas of your life. Keep practicing them daily please. Your today is creating your tomorrow.

Life really is all about the practice. In this chapter, I'm going to guide you to create your own, easily repeatable assortment of self-care practices that will keep you on track to consistently feeling better. Practices to practice. You *can* do it. I know you can. I'm not giving up on you, so please don't give up on yourself!

I'm going to list and describe *some* (not all) self-care, feel better practices, and activities, that you can consider and choose to create your own personal plan to a happier and healthier life. Everyone is different, so you get to choose activities and practices that line up with *you*. Here's the catch: You have to *do* them! You can't watch someone else work out at the gym and expect to gain the benefits yourself. Right? Right. But the good news is that you're choosing practices that feel good and that support *you*. What's not to like? It's your own personal self-care workout to keep you healthier and vital.

Did you get that word? *Vital*. Yes, it's vital. It's not just a good idea. How badly do you want to feel better and make some positive changes in your life? Because you have to *want* it. When you want something different, you can't keep doing the same thing. Expecting a different outcome doesn't make sense, right?

Any change for the better requires your *will* to change. Wishing for change or just thinking about it without action won't do it. It takes your decision to change what you believe, what you think, how you feel, and what you do. It takes your commitment. How committed would you be if what you did saved the life of someone you love right now? OK, look in a mirror now. See that best friend who has been through it *all* with you? Now look again, and see that future you that you are creating today. How you care for yourself today makes a difference, and *you* are worth it. Love you. Commit.

Besides your *will* and *commitment*, you will also get the best result with *consistency*. I know, this sounds harder now, but it's really not. Hard is sitting in the mud and choosing to stay there. It will just take repetition and practice. The more you practice something, the more it becomes a habit or a practice. Bathing and brushing your teeth are practices that have become routine—I hope. So just think of it as adding some healthy habits for your greater good.

Yes, you'll likely begin and continue your personal daily disciplines for a while and then forget or get distracted and fall off the grid. That's OK. No one is perfect. This isn't about perfection. This is about *you* taking care of yourself—no guilt, no shame. But if you get derailed for too long and stop your self-care, you may soon notice that you just don't feel as well. You may notice that you are more irritable or reactive or less tolerant. You might resume less productive patterns that you were wanting to change. Somehow, life isn't going as smoothly.

This is your reminder to get back on track and return to your self-care practices and routines. Pick them back up and continue on. When you've scraped your knees enough times and you're tired of it, your *will* to change becomes stronger. When your *will* is strong, you will do what you choose to do. Are you sick and tired of feeling sick and tired? If you are, it's time for a change. Walk this way.

Your Plan

Here are several practices for you to consider and expand on. You get to choose which ones to add to your plan of daily disciplines to improve your life. You can alter it at any time. You may choose certain activities on certain days or adjust per your life schedule and body time clock. I wouldn't compare yourself to anyone else's routines; just do what fits you. Life will cause interruptions, but just get back to what keeps you feeling your best and moving in a direction that you prefer. Here they are:

Gratitude. Feeling and practicing gratitude is one of the quickest ways to change and improve how you feel and your overall attitude. Begin by thinking of and listing those people (yourself included), things, circumstances, and experiences that you appreciate in your life. Look around and think, *Thank you for... Thank you that I have... Thank you that I am...* Remember, it's important to *feel* what you are noticing and listing. When you *feel* gratitude and appreciation, you are literally raising your energy. You'll feel it. It only takes a few minutes. You can tack it on to making your bed, washing dishes, doing yardwork, or driving. I recommend starting and ending your day in gratitude. It will prepave your day and evening. This upliftment is natural medicine. It's also free and has no negative side effects.

Meditation, Mindfulness, and Prayer. Meditation is just getting quiet and still and more open. Mindfulness is becoming more aware of and relaxing into the present moment. We often live unconsciously on autopilot. We get caught up in the hustle and bustle of our lives. To become mindful, just stop your work and notice how you are feeling, what you are doing, and your environment. Stop, listen, and feel. It just takes a few moments to check in. It may even lead to some gratitude. When you quiet your thoughts and the world around you, you are more receptive to your own inner guidance and intuition. Prayer is a communion and conversation with God/your higher power. All three practices can take many forms. Meditation can be as simple as shifting your attention to and noticing your breaths. You can sit and listen to a recorded meditation or music, or you can take a walk in nature and listen to the birds. You could also go to the Himalayas if you want, but you don't need to. You can do it anywhere you can find and create peace. Just do it. You can start your practice with gratitude to release the day and elevate your energy. Settle in your heart, and enjoy some peace. You can send prayers at the end if you wish. There are many meditation resources in the world. Try different ways and choose what you prefer. The Calm app is good, and it's not long. The health benefits of these practices are many. These include a reduction in stress and anxiety, which contribute to inflammation and the negative cascade of potential health conditions and diseases. They promote improved sleep, peace, happiness, clear thinking, and greater states of acceptance and well-being.

Vision of my life. Here's where that Do Want list comes in. Pull it out, and review what you would prefer in all areas of your life. Feel how each of them *feels* for twenty to thirty seconds. Smile and hold the list in your heart. Before you know it, you will have memorized your list. Leave out the worry or overthinking about when or how things will work out. Simply say, "This or something better, please and thank you." Then let it go and move on with your day. Ask God/the Universe to help you to recognize your next steps as they come to you. Easy, happy medicine. You can take this medicine once, twice, or three times a day.

Healthy habits. This includes many self-care practices that I mentioned previously. Regular healthy nutrition and supplements, exercise, sleep, and energy practices fit in here. Self-directed Compassion Key is a great healthy habit to release any tensions or negative emotions and to replace them with your truth and positive statements and emotions. Also, a routine checkup with your health-care provider is a good idea to objectively assess your health-care needs and optimize your overall health.

Social time. We are not meant to be alone. We feel better and live healthier lives when we are in social contact with others. Choose your degree of interaction, but take time to share life with family, friends, and coworkers. Join a group or a cause in which you can find like-minded people. It's important to relate, share, laugh, cry, and enjoy a range of experiences with others. We grow as individuals through relationships. We learn things about ourselves and others and expand our ability to express and receive compassion. This promotes our health and well-being.

Hobbies, creativity, and fun. What do you like and love to do? If you aren't sure, take a few moments to think about it. Life gets busy, and sometimes we can forget what we used to like to do. Maybe what we like to do has changed. For example, do you like to bike, swim, walk, hike, climb, boat, or participate in certain sports? Do you like to make or fix things, dance, play or listen to music, create artwork, or read? Do you like to go out to a show or travel? Watching television isn't all bad, but it is more of a pastime. Include those personal hobbies and outlets that you enjoy in your life. It works best if you put them on the list on purpose and make them happen. Doing what you like and love elevates your energy. It's a win-win.

Positive mindset and affirming statements. The power of a more positive mindset cannot be overstated. So much has been written and spoken about this topic. Focusing on and being grateful for what you *do* have and what *is* going right elevates your energy and your spirit. That positivity needs to also be pointed inward to and for yourself. Self-love and appreciation are acts of love for God/the Universe, of which you are a part. What part of God isn't good enough or is unworthy of appreciation? None. Your confidence is actually rooted in your true inner self, not in your smaller, life-story perception of who you think you are. Remember the truth of who you are, and let this guide you in forming a list of positive, affirming statements that begin with "I am..." The words you place after these two words are very important. Your mind is listening. Your personal I-am statements are very powerful in rewiring your beliefs and in creating every part of your life. You can search and find many different affirmation audios online; short and long. Write your own statements and say them out loud. You *are* who you *say* you are. Keep it positive. Here are some examples: "I am... healthy, enough, brave, strong, kind, hopeful, worthy, grateful, a good friend, a hard worker, safe, capable, determined, happy, improving, content, love, abundant, a piece of God/the Universe, a healthy habit person." A positive, self-loving mindset is nourishing medicine for the soil from which you are creating your life.

Forgiveness. Forgiveness is a healthy practice? Yes, it is. Forgiveness for yourself and for others releases the ties that bind you to negative emotions. When you forgive, you see the problems or injustices and the pain that occurred, but you stop carrying them around with you in your backpack of pain. You may have heard it said that unforgiveness is like drinking poison and hoping the other person (the one who hurt you) will die. Unforgiveness hurts the one who chooses not to forgive. The quicker you can forgive, the quicker the cords of attachment are cut between the offended and the offender. Getting trusted counsel may help the process of forgiveness. There are many ways to work through it. It may take time, or it may go more quickly than you might think. To address forgiveness, I include the simple statements of the Ho'oponopono prayer[42] in my daily disciplines. This is an ancient Hawaiian prayer that has been used for healing, forgiveness, reconciliation, inner peace, and self-love. I like things that get a lot done! The prayer loosely translates as: "to make it right again." It's about taking responsibility for everything that shows up in your life. Often, what we see as a problem outside of ourselves is an opportunity within us to resolve and heal what is ready to be addressed. The prayer has four simple statements. They may be said in any order. This is what I say:

- I love you.
- I'm sorry.
- Please forgive me.
- Thank you.

You simply repeat these phrases to yourself, to others in your life or the world, and to whatever circumstance you would like. These words encourage a state of inner healing that allows you to accept what is and move to a more peaceful and more positive place. You can feel better, let go, and let God assist you in returning to your natural state of well-being. As we do this for ourselves, we do it for others. One piece affects the other. Forgiveness is medicine for all of us! (Resources for the Ho'oponopono prayer are listed at the end of the book.)

Make Your Lists!

OK, now you can pick and choose your *own*, easily repeatable daily disciplines from these lists, and you can add more of your own. Create and write your list on paper or notecards to post where you will see it. You can also keep your list on a tablet, computer, or phone. You can set an alarm to remind yourself to start your gratitude, vision for my life, or meditation/prayer practices. You can check them off as you complete them if that feels good. You can set a pattern to include certain activities on even or odd days or to do certain disciplines on Monday, Wednesday, and Friday.

As you find what works best for you and keep repeating it, your new way of doing life will become second nature. You can change your routine as you like. Your new and improved way of feeling and living your life has been set into motion, so keep it going.

One day you will stop and realize" *Hmmm... I feel better!* Smile and give yourself a pat on the back or a hug. You made it happen. If you get distracted, it's OK. Just get back up and continue your disciplines. It's a practice and a process of self-care and feeling better. It's not hard, and you are so worth it!

Wow! I can see the way *out* of the maze just ahead. Let's step through to the other side!...You go first...I'm right behind you.

It's so clear and bright here and feels like *peace* and *freedom*. I hope you think and feel that it's been worth every turn that we've made and all of the steps that we've taken to get here. One more pearl to collect, and then we'll string them all together to add to your life collections. We'll see how far we've come in the next and final chapter. Move on, free and clear, when you are ready.

Musical Offering

"Bulletproof" by Citizen Way
"Cheer You On" by Jordan Feliz
"Overcomer" by Mandisa
"One Nation Under a Groove" by Funkadelic

Pearl

Your daily disciplines of self-love and self-care are your stepping stones out of the maze of life to a happier and healthier you.

CHAPTER 9

Your New You!

Here you are. You made it! You're now near the end of your journey from where you *were* in your awareness and understandings to a place with a *new* perspective and outlook. From prior patterns and habits of thinking and feeling to being more open to changing them for the better. From patterns of negative emotions to opening your heart with self-love and compassion to heal and release what you are ready to let go.

You've traveled from a place of feeling stuck or disheartened by the struggles of life to a more solid footing. You will feel better here, and you will be better able to manage the waves of your life. Yes, there will still be waves, but you now have some new ways to lessen their effects and to ride them to a better place.

You have also washed off some of the mud that kept you stuck and obscured your vision for an improved way of living.

Like Dorothy from *The Wizard of Oz*, you have remembered that you are *not* lost or alone. You have learned some methods and have picked up some tools (and pearls) to help you *think* more clearly, as dear Scarecrow was able to experience. And like Tin Man who had lost *heart* along the way, love and compassion can prevail. In the end, even Lion traded worry- and fear-based thoughts for truth and *courage*. The monkeys and the Wicked Witch of the West may show up in your life, but now, instead of reacting in fear, you can remember who you are and pick up your bucket of tools and douse and melt them with your disciplines of self-love, self-compassion, and self-care. You are not the same.

Dear one, your *beliefs* can contribute to health conditions and diseases, or they can reduce or resist their occurrence. Becoming more aware of your beliefs and thoughts and then learning to manage how you feel is critical to your complete health and well-being.

Your *thoughts* and *feelings* are your medicines. Your *self-love* and *compassion* are your medicines. Your daily disciplines of healthy *self-care* are your medicines. You *do* have choices. Your inner state reflects to your outer physical body. Everything is connected. *You* are your best medicine. Your body will do what your mind believes.

Commonly, it is our unconscious guilt and a lack of self-acceptance and self-love that promote health conditions, illness, and disease. Sometimes the illness will point symbolically to what needs healing. Self-love, forgiveness, and compassion can heal the obstacles to wellness and well-being. When we can choose to let go of the obstacles and realize our true inner selves, there is peace and there is love.

> The body is within the mind.
> —Sir David R. Hawkins, MD

When you realize peace and love, you also realize **you** are your source of happiness, health, and well-being. When you address the impressions you are ready to release or heal, you can create what you would prefer from your **wellness**. It's your inner connection to your truth and your state of peace that are your best fuels for the medicines you flow into your body and out into your life. You are a powerful creator.

Follow *your* path and return home to your inner truth, strength, and well-being. As with our dear Dorothy, your ticket home was always with you. You just needed to click your heels together and knock off some of the mud on your ruby slippers to see the love that you are! *You* are love. Create your life from love.

I'm sending *my* love and prayers for *you* and your health, happiness, and well-being! Now keep moving, dear one...

Dr. Sheila Balestrino

Musical Offering

"I'm Coming Out" by Diana Ross
"Wildflowers" by Tom Petty
"You Can Do It" by One Way
(Go ahead and dance!)

Pearl

You can do it!
(Oh yes, you can!)

You Are...

... Free!

REFERENCES AND RESOURCES BY CHAPTER

Chapter 1

1. Deepak Chopra M.D. Connect with this physician, author, spiritual teacher and speaker @ DeepakChopra.com, Chopra Global and the app, YouTube videos, and meditations, and podcasts.
2. Esther Hicks Abraham-Hicks publications.com—Art of Allowing video (Upstream vs Downstream).—Hicks, Esther and Jerry, The Astonishing Power of Emotions, let your feelings be your guide. United States: Hay House, Inc. 2007. ISBN 978-1-4019-1246-8.

Chapter 2

3. Dr. Wayne W. Dyer. A renowned author and public speaker on personal and spiritual development worth remembering.☺ His wisdom lives on in written, audio and video forms. HayHouse.com provides many of his works. 15 Life-Changing Lessons To Learn From Wayne Dyer is @ purposefairy.com.
4. The Wizard of Oz (1939 film) United States: Warner Brothers.
5. Tolle, Eckhart, A New Earth. United States: Penguin Books, 2016. ISBN 978-0-452-28996-3.—Eckharttolle.com for all of his resources.
6. Panache Desai. Panachedesai.com for his resources and his daily Call To Calm support and meditations.
7. Anita Moorjani. Anitamoorjani.com. for her resources.—Moorjani, Anita, Dying To Be Me. United States: Hay House, Inc., 2012. ISBN 978-1-4019-3753-9.
8. Cohen, Alan, A Course In Miracles made easy. United States: Hay House, Inc., 2015. ISBN 978-1-4019-4734-7. Grab a copy ☺ also @ www.AlanCohen.com. for his resources.

Chapter 3

9. Moorjani, Anita, Dying To Be Me. United States: Hay House, Inc., 2015. pp 148-48. ISBN 978-1-4019-4734-7.
10. Louise Hay. Hay, Louise L., You Can Heal Your Life. United States: Hay House, Inc., 1999. p 33. ISBN 1-56170-628-0.
11. Rev. Lorraine Cohen. In loving memory, Lorraine@lorrainecohen.com. 12/2/2014.
12. Joel F. Wade Ph.D. Wade Ph.D., Joel F., New Ideas for Living Well, jwade@drjoelwade.com, 1/29/2018. Use this email for his resources like his book: Happiness is a Virtue, and his audio course: Mastering Happiness. He also has a podcast.

Chapter 4

13. Marisa Peer. marisapeer.com for all of her resources including the book: I Am Enough, and her Rapid Transitional Therapy.
14. Neale Donald Walsch. www.nealedonaldwalsch.com for all of his books, audios, and resources.
15. The Emotional Guidance Scale. Image from Not 9 to 5 Org on Facebook. General resource: Abraham-Hicks Publications.

Chapter 5

16. Compassion Key. Compassionkey.com.
17. DrSheilaBalestrino.com

Chapter 6

18. Chopra M.D., Deepak and Tanzi Ph.D., Rudolph E., The Healing Self. United States: Harmony Books, 2018. P 89. ISBN 978-0-451-49552-5.
19. Lipton PH.D., Bruce H., The Biology Of Belief. United States: Hay House, Inc., 2015. p 139-40, 55, 219. ISBN 978-1-4019-4891-7.
20. Chopra M.D., Deepak and Tanzi Ph.D., Rudolph E.,2015. p 135.
21. The Mediterranean Diet. Resources: www.healthline.com, www.mayoclinic.org, www.webmd.com.
22. Unhealthy fats. Lisa Balestrino, MS, RD, LDN, CSSD.

23. Anti-inflammatory diet. Resources: www.webmd.com, www.medicalnewstoday.com, www.everydayhealth.com, www.healthline.com.
24. Superfoods. www.runnersworld.com/best/superfoods, www.healthline.com.
25. Fee radicals. https/www.mayoclinic.org, 11/23/2019.,
26. blog.bulletproof.com/best anti-aging superfoods, 7 Most Powerful Anti-Aging Superfoods., 7/9/2019.
27. Robbins, Ocean, 31-Day Food Revolution. United States: Grand Central Publishing, 2019. ISBN 9781538746257.
28. Greenmedinfo.com.
29. Hyman M.D., Mark, The Pegan Diet. United States: Little, Brown Spark, 2021. ISBN 978-0-316-53708-7.
30. Asprey, Dave, Fast This Way. United States: HarperCollins, 2021. ISBN 9780062882868.
31. Microbiome. www.healthline.com, www.webmd.com, Gundrymd.com., www.webmd.com.
32. Leaky Gut. Campos M.D., Marcelo, Leaky Gut: What is it, and what does it mean to you?. Harvard Health Publishing, Harvard Medical School. 10/22/2019. www.webmd.com. www.healthline.com. Centerfordigestivediseases.com.
33. Viome. Viome.com.
34. Exercise. Fulghum Bruce PhD., Debra, Exercise and Depression. WebMd. 2/18/2020., Webmd.com.
35. Exercise. https://medlineplus.gov/benefitsofexercise.html., Benefits of Exercise. 8/27/21.
36. Exercise.https//medlineplus.gov/howmuchexercisedoineed.html. How much exercise do I need? 8/25/21.
37. Sleep. Sleepfoundation.org. Leech MS, Joe, 10 Reasons Why Good Sleep Is Important. 2/24/2020. www.healthline.com.
38. Asprey, Dave, Game Changers. United States: HarperCollins, 2018. p 137. ISBN 978-0-06-265244-7.
39. Micheal Breus Ph.D. www.thesleepdoctor.com. www.thepowerofwhenquiz.com.
40. Toxins. Complete list-Environmental Toxins, Top 10 common Household Toxins. www.time.com.

Chapter 7

41. Quantum-success-coaching-academy.com.

Chapter 8

42. The Ho'oponopono Prayer. Vitale, Joe, Zero Limits. United States: John Wiley & Sons, Inc., 2007. ISBN 978-0-470-10147-6.

Other Resources to Consider

Dr. Joe Dispenza
Gregg Braden
Gabrielle Bernstein
Lewis Howes
David R. Hawkins
Christy Whitman
Beth Herndobler
Tammy Mastroberte
Matt Khan
Debra Poneman
Humanitys Team
Gaia
Carol Tuttle

Gundry MD
Dr. Furhman
BioTrust
Revelation Health
Farmers Juice
Elysium Health
Mindbodygreen
Ka'Chava

Printed in the United States
by Baker & Taylor Publisher Services